POWER S

POWER SELLING

Realize your sales potential

Michael Friedman
and Jeffrey Weiss

Thorsons
An Imprint of HarperCollins*Publishers*

Thorsons
An Imprint of Harper-Collins*Publishers*
77–85 Fulham Palace Road,
Hammersmith, London W6 8JB

First published by Tern Enterprises 1986
Thorsons edition published in one volume 1989

3 5 7 9 10 8 6 4

© Tern Enterprises 1986, 1989

A catalogue record for this book
is available from the British Library

ISBN 0 7225 1922 2

Printed in Great Britain by Hartnolls Ltd., Cornwall

CONTENTS

THE PHILOSOPHY OF POWER SELL

PART ONE: POWER SELL

PART TWO: COLD CALLS, HOT LEADS AND POWER PROSPECTING

PART THREE: POWER PHONING

PART FOUR: CLOSING THE SALE

PART FIVE: PERSONAL POWER SELL

PART SIX: POWER SELLING
TO GROUPS

The Philosophy of Power Sell

Power Sell is based on a simple, exciting truth: **You, the individual salesman, are better at your profession than you think you are.**

Sure, there are some selling tips you might not know about yet—and they're here by the score, scattered helpfully throughout this book.

But the bottom-line message that makes Power Selling work for so many successful, high-income salesmen is directed straight at *you*.

First of all, together we're going to **find the specific strengths and specific weaknesses** that make you the unique salesman you are.

Next we're going to show you how you can **turn up the power** *full blast* on those characteristic strengths: how to focus on what you do best; how to aim for the most productive use of your talents; how to intensify, with pride and passion, the qualities that naturally brought you into the challenging and rewarding profession of selling.

Then we'll talk about dealing with those **qualities that might look like weaknesses.** Power Selling is an approach based on facing the truth: how to turn negative factors, once recognized, into powerfully positive qualities; how to take command of the sales situation so that strong, not weak, points will take control; how to play to your strengths.

These are books about getting *influence,* and making it work for you. About getting the customer to take his buying cues from you. About bringing customer interest to a white-hot boil. And about **turning selling into co-operation**—with the customer eager for you to help him buy.

It works! It can put you in control of that vital element, the sales close. And that, in turn, can change your career—and your ideas about yourself. So turn the page, and see how power—in its most positive sense—will put **you** at the top!

PART ONE: POWER SELL

INTRODUCTION TO PART ONE

People tell me not to fight, but they are at the foot of the wall of knowledge, and I am at the top. My horizon is greater than theirs. . . . People need challenges.
—Muhammad Ali

Introduction to Part One

Where does it come from, that desire to succeed? To outdo—not just other people at your level—but your own track record to date?

The hunger for achievement that impelled a political outsider past retirement age to become the most powerful leader in the world; that fired a stunt-man, bit player and failed writer to become international movie stars; that led an executive dismissed by Henry Ford II to become a $1,000,000-a-year corporation president, best-selling author and shadow candidate for President of the United States—well, what Ronald Reagan, Burt Reynolds, Clint Eastwood, Sylvester Stallone and Lee Iacocca have—wherever they got it—was the determination to reach the top.

They had to sell themselves, just as *you* will have to sell *your*self, if you're reading this book because you want to become a better salesman. They found self-confidence when most people "in the know" had written them off as failures, or has-beens. (You don't have to be too elderly to remember when Reagan was ridiculed as a forgotten B-movie actor who never got the girl in pictures and was too old and out of the mainstream to make a respectable showing in a national election. As for Stallone, when nobody would hire him for a major part, he'd simply sit down and write a script in which he starred. Your children and grandchildren may *still* be seeing the latest sequel in the Rocky series.)

This is remarkable success, but it is not success without an explanation. People who struggle to achieve have learned a simple lesson:

> *You have to have the power to*
> *continue, no matter what the*
> *setbacks. You have to find within*
> *yourself the courage and obstinacy*
> *to keep fighting.*

"Power selling" is an approach to marketing, to moving products, to convincing another human being that he or she needs and desires what you are selling.

But it's more. Fundamentally, power selling is based upon your ability to let yourself face an essential truth:

> *You are better than anyone else*
> *thinks you are.*

Think about it. Unless someone has just agreed to guarantee you a salary of £30,000 a month or has given you the keys to a hillside mansion in Spain, the world is not forking over any testimonial to your hidden value, right?

You are getting what you earn. You get paid when you deliver. And that arrangement is not going to change in your lifetime—unless you happen to win the lottery or someone discovers a uranium deposit beneath your front lawn. **People will pay you what you earn, not what you are worth.**

So, you have to find within yourself the conviction

that you are worth. . .well, what? A life that revolves around two homes, a life marked by long periods of free time, a job at the centre of the action, a huge bank account? That, too, you have to decide for yourself—not only what you're worth, but *how* you want it.

What's your game plan? Without a strategy, all your effort and all your self-confidence will go scattershot. You won't benefit from this book and the step-by-step hints outlined in it unless you take a moment to:

1) Decide for yourself what you are worth, and
2) Decide exactly how you want to be compensated for that worth.

Take an example. You're selling condominiums right now, pulling down an average of £15,000 to £20,000 a year. But you look around at some of your peers, or at the guys at the top of the company, or at some of the customers you're dealing with, and something seems wrong with the numbers. Are you getting cheated? No, you're just not taking advantage of your full potential. If you're worth more than, say, Harry or George, then it's up to you, and *no one else,* to make sure that you begin to make the opportunities that will lead to your making more money than Harry or George.

And don't waste too much time trying to figure out how they're doing so well. Learn what you can, by their example, and then move on. (And if Harry's so comfortable because he married the boss's daughter, just grin and forget it. You can't take his route, unless your state has no laws against bigamy, and there's no point in tightening up your insides with envy or resentment.)

> *Determine what you are worth, but*
> *don't get hung up on what other*
> *people are not worth.*

Okay, decide what you're worth. Say, only £50,000 a
year (because you're just getting used to the idea of as-
sessing yourself at full market value!). Now, there's
step two: You have to decide how that worth is going to
be expressed. And this is harder than you think, because, if you're like most people, you've probably
taken too much for granted.

Do you have to work for somebody else? Is it necessary that you stay in one place, or, depending upon your
likes and dislikes, is it necessary that you travel on the
road? Do you want to live in the country, or the city, or
both? Do you want freedom or security? Chances are
you've been so busy doing the actual work of selling
day in and day out (and trying to have some time for
your personal life), that you haven't stepped back and
asked yourself just what you really want from your job.

Burt Reynolds knew. A prematurely bald, relatively
short stunt man who was told that he looked like a poor
man's Marlon Brando, Reynolds knew he wanted to be
a star known for good looks, good humour and good
grace, and he knew that he wanted to be able to live well
and devote his life to acting. He did it.

Lee Iacocca knew, even after he had been fired by the

most influential man in his industry and was in the enviable position of living out a cozy retirement.

Clint Eastwood knew. And it's time you knew, right? **What are you worth? And how do you want to get compensated by the world out there?**

When you're clear on those two basic points, you're that much closer to tapping your own unique power. You have to have the goal, and then you have to take the most useful attitude: the can-do approach.

"There are so many opportunities," says Armand Hammer, chairman of Occidental Petroleum Corporation, "but people don't always know how to take advantage of them. You have to be willing to take risks. You need courage. That's very important. You can't be afraid of things."

This is the advice of a man who is not only wealthy but politically powerful as well. But the *real* power that was important to him came in the beginning—not power over others, but power over himself and power in the daily challenges that face anyone who has a personal vision of success.

And it isn't easy. It takes tremendous reserves of power, as you already know, to keep going day after day in the face of possible defeat. It *is* easier to sit back and take the ordinary routes. And why not?

> *Power selling is an approach that*
> *can inspire you, but it can exhaust*
> *you as well.*

You have to have the strength to keep coming back for more. You have to have the unusual kind of determination that characterizes a winner. You have to turn a deaf ear to the argument that there's nothing all that bad about living a life in the slow lane—enough to eat, enough for the family needs, something left over for vacations and entertainment, a couple of luxury items, security, and so on.

Nothing wrong with that kind of life, as millions of people will tell you (and don't they sound as if they really mean it?)—but if you want more out of your life and your career, you may have to develop the power to keep going when your best friends urge you to give up ...the power to return again and again to the scene of what looks like defeat...the power to show the world what you're really worth, **and make the world pay you for it!**

In Part One:

- You're going to be reminded of the importance of getting yourself turned on to the whole sales process.

- You're going to learn the basics of firing up the customer.

- There'll be an explanation of the "Five Cardinal Don'ts."

- You'll also read about the difference between the "order taker" and the "order *maker*"

- And then there'll be a quick summary of the essentials of power selling.

Introduction to Part One

You should read this over and over. It only takes a few minutes the first time through. The concepts are not so difficult to understand. But the message behind them may take more time to digest, time to become part of your natural behaviour.

So keep it around, say, for those extra few minutes of down time when you're waiting to see a busy customer and when you just might be starting to feel a little insecure or unimportant...or for those depressing delays late at night in a busy airport, when you just might be wondering if it's all going to lead anywhere...then turn to a chapter that inspired you once, and **let the ideas of power selling get you going again.**

Repeat the lessons here until they become second nature, until you begin achieving at the level you're after. And then you might want to pass it along to a friend (provided he's not in the same business).

Power selling, if you work at it, if you believe in yourself, can put you on top. And isn't that where you belong?

CHAPTER ONE
Turn-on Rules

I want to play all the time. I think the mark of a good player is his consistency. And the only way a guy can be consistent is to play all the time.

—Pete Rose

Turn-on Rules

You have to love it; that's the first element in power selling. That doesn't mean you don't feel the butterflies fluttering in your stomach when you face an important customer, or that you don't have moments of severe self-doubt.

Fear is natural, and no successful person is a stranger to it. Let's face it—when you aim to move ahead of the crowd, you become an exposed target.

But you can transform the adrenalin of nervousness into energy, and the secret to doing that is reminding yourself that you love selling.

The power within power selling
comes from enjoying the test!

As you've heard thousands of times, selling is like acting, and the greatest actors of all time admit to stage fright. And why not? A career is on the line, people will be carefully watching to see whether the actor succeeds or fails, and, when the curtain goes up, there's no turning back!

Well, you're in a similar situation every time you face a customer, because the word goes out. Your performance will reverberate, and it will be remembered. You won't usually have a second chance.

But these are the negative ways of looking at a moment of opportunity. Tap into your individual feelings of power, let them surge to the fore, and you'll see it all in "can-do reverse":

*The opportunity to be disgraced
is also the opportunity to impress
the world, and the risk of failure
is also the possibility of tremendous
success.*

The audience (to recall the first rule of entertainment) *wants* to be entertained. Who buys a ticket at today's prices in order to be bored or annoyed? Your customer, too, wants to be sold to; otherwise, he's put himself in the position of wasting time.

Uh-oh. You may have found that hard to take, but consider it a moment: **The customer wants to be sold to.** It's not always true, and any estate agent can tell you about the kind of customer who just wants to look round houses every weekend; but most people, most of the time, if they've allowed themselves to be within your reach, are hoping that you have something they want. Yes, that's true the large majority of the time. (And when it isn't true, where's the harm in acting as if it is? You get better in your job, and you might even win a sale, to the customer's surprise!)

Never forget this basic fact. Just as an audience might look unresponsive to a frightened actor (because he has low self-esteem, or because they might be tired or uncertain about what's coming), your customer might look only mildly interested. In fact, as a defence against unpleasantly aggressive salesmanship, the customer might pretend lack of interest in the extreme.

But the customer has come into the showroom, let you into the house, or has given you an appointment by choice. **The customer chose you!** Take that attitude, and you're on the right track at the beginning. *You've been chosen! The opportunity is yours!*

TURN-ON RULE 1

And this, by the way, is what makes you enjoy your work, just as Pete Rose enjoys hitting singles: the chance to do what you do best. So here's our first Turn-on Rule:

> *The customer wants it!*

Once you see the truth of that simple rule, you'll feel the butterflies calm down, because you will realize that, from the first, you really are in the power position.

Unfortunately, all too many people in sales have a nagging fear that they'll become pale copies of poor Willie Loman, the defeated salesman in Arthur Miller's "Death of a Salesman." They think they have to plead, beg, grovel. But the title of the play should be read in more than one way: The "death" of the salesman occurs before this man dies; he died as a salesman when he lost faith in his ability to sell, when he let failure take away his sense of self-worth and personal dignity. He lost sight of what you must always remember and believe in your bones:

> *The salesperson performs an*
> *important service.*

Sales keep the country moving, keep the economy strong. Everyone benefits from that, of course.

On the personal level, however (where you will be operating most of the time), the importance of a salesperson is to benefit individual lives. Some people will tell you that a sale is a confrontation, and that you must somehow defeat the customer to make a sale.

Yes, that takes a kind of power. But the kind of power selling we recommend is very different. It's based on the belief that **you are the customer's *guide*, not an adversary;** you are, in the true sense of the expression, performing a service.

TURN-ON RULE 2

And so we go from the first Turn-on Rule to the second, which is based upon the conviction that you are a salesperson because you like people and you like yourself. Tap into your sense of power, but also tap into the power generated by the needs and wishes of the potential customer. *What a combination, if you get it right!*

Here's our second Turn-on Rule:

You can *satisfy the customer!*

The customer wants something, and you can fulfill that want. Without this attitude, you're going to be in real trouble. And what can this attitude lead to but enjoyment of your work? When you get up in the morning, even though there will be occasional days when your

Turn-on Rules

sales future looks greyer than you'd like, you can usually look in the mirror and say, "Today, I am going to have the chance to do something for somebody else. I'm going to help someone with a problem or help someone fulfill a fantasy or help someone find the gift that gives pleasure to a loved one. I can do something important for someone else, and that's important for me."

Tape that thought to your mirror, in your own words. It's not self-delusion; it's the prescription for the attitude you need. It's the thought to remember when you're attacked by those butterflies.

Or perhaps you should recall the words of golfer Lee Trevino, whose smooth and gentlemanly demeanour most of us would envy: "I may be laughing on the outside and seething on the inside. It's what's happening on the inside that gives me my drive, my motivation."

Inside, ambition may gnaw at you, you may be humanly fearful that you aren't doing as well as you could be, but you should let the customer see nothing but **calm, courtesy, commitment— the three C's of professional sales attitudes.**

After all, the customer is going to respond to th. salesperson who's turned on to his or her own talents and potential. . .or at least gives the appearance of being so. Before hitting the sales floor or entering a client's office, flash a quick picture in your mind: **I, the power seller, in full-colour video!** Watch yourself *as you want to see yourself,* standing tall and exuding confidence, glowing with health and moving with restraint.

In a few minutes, you will be concentrating all your energies and concentration upon someone else, so this little reminder is important, a last-minute inspection of the image that you've decided to project. That image, by the way, should be closer to Roger Moore than Rambo, despite all the books you might read suggesting that you bring full fire-power to bear upon a hapless customer.

But it is critical that you choose an image that suits you, that brings out the best in you, that is fuelled from within, that you believe in...even if it *is* Rambo, after all. The point is to be convincing, not astonishing. Keep your image firmly in mind. Let it be a challenge.

TURN-ON RULE 3

Our third Turn-on Rule is:

> *Don't just be yourself—magnify and*
> *intensify yourself!*

You are worth selling, just as your product is worth selling. You have nothing to hide; you have everything to show. The power of your sales presentation will be augmented by your presentation of yourself as an individual. *Warning:* That doesn't mean you brag about your golf scores or your children's high marks; it does mean that you appreciate yourself sensibly, as a sales professional.

Whatever your personal virtues and achievements,

you are well within your rights to let the customer know subtly but firmly that you know what you're doing. You have the calm of someone who's on top of the situation, or so you must project...you are courteous but not self-effacing, because you have the dignity of someone who believes in the job to be done, and so you project ...you have the commitment of someone who is totally concentrated on making a sale—not just *any* sale, but the sale that will benefit both you and your customer.

There's a moment of truth when you and the customer face each other. The split second of the first impression may be half the battle, if you handle it right. Make it the best cut possible from your imaginary video: *You in action!*

TURN-ON RULE 4

Remember the good times!

Most of us can find a rush of power in remembering a past success, but we forget to turn to that source when we need it most.

If you're new in sales, you might not have a particular sale to recall, but you've had other types of success. You don't need to be told which moments are the most helpful: It's those times when you felt on top of the world because you achieved more than you expected, when everything fell into place because you had *made* it happen. Draw upon those memories.

You may be about to face the most formidable customer in your area, or perhaps the person who just walked into your showroom looks as if she would rather suffer spontaneous combustion than buy anything she sees for sale—but what about that other time, when you . . . (fill in the blanks)?

Sure, there are things to be learned from failure, but don't forget what can be learned from success.

If you've done it before, you can do it again.

When you and the customer meet, what will be playing in your brain? "Hi, I'm the salesperson who hasn't made a sale all day," or "Hi, I'm the super salesperson who sold two TV sets to that couple who were 'just looking' the other day"? What's going on in your brain shows on your face, in the way you walk, in the sound of your voice—so it had better be positive, if you want to make a good impression.

Power comes from playing to strength. You are energized, literally, by success. A conscious appeal to the memory of past success will invigorate you as you face the toughest prospect on your list. It may even put a smile on your face that unmistakably announces to all the world, "Hey, I'm really good at what I do." And it will charge you up for the challenge.

We've been talking about the importance of finding your sources of individual power and tapping them for the best results, but you don't operate in a vacuum. There's one final ingredient that's crucial in revving yourself up for efficient salesmanship. That's right: *the product*. Power selling depends upon your belief in the product you're determined to sell.

Oh, you could become a successful salesperson selling snake oil, if you really worked at it, but what a useless diversion of important energy! You'd be squandering your reserves of power on duping the customer, on hiding what you really knew to be true, on hoping that you could avoid dealing with the inevitable complaints. What a waste.

TURN-ON RULE 5

Instead, take a look at this:

Believe, or recant!

In other words, if you can't develop a commitment to your product based on certain knowledge that customers will be satisfied with it and grateful to you, then you abandon that product and find another.

Sounds impossible? Are sales jobs so difficult to find in your area that you feel stuck with representing an inferior or unsound product or service? Then you'd better find another profession, fast, because you're setting yourself up for nothing but lack of self-respect and dislike of your work.

No, power selling at its most intense and effective requires that you gain power from belief in what you are selling. You have to believe in yourself; and you can't do that fully unless you believe in what you sell, because you and the product are a team.

Perhaps you have not really taken enough time or thought to choose the right product to represent. Perhaps that didn't seem so important when you were first starting out. *But it is the product that does half your work for you (if it's worthwhile), and belief in the product gives you pride in your efforts.*

If you are not a believer, customers will catch on soon enough. For unrestricted access to the powers within you, you cannot let yourself be hampered by a grudging commitment to shoddy goods or undependable services.

Forget any myth you've heard about the salesperson who can sell anything, no matter how superfluous. You will be at your best when you sincerely feel a commitment to what you're selling. **Believe in yourself; believe in your product or service. That will give you a double power.**

TELL YOURSELF AGAIN

Next, we're going to talk about using power selling to fire up the customer. Let him or her have the full blast of your self-confidence and commitment. But first, a review of the ideas you must memorize and repeat until they become second nature to the way you think, feel and operate:

1) The customer wants to be sold. Take that attitude, and he'll be swept along with it! THE CUSTOMER WANTS IT!

Turn-on Rules

2) You know how to do your job so that it's a professional service. You can help the customer in your own skilled way. YOU *CAN* SATISFY THE CUSTOMER!

3) You are your own best product. Turn on the bright lights, because there are no cracks or flaws! DON'T JUST BE YOURSELF—MAGNIFY AND INTENSIFY YOURSELF!

4) Build on the past. Let those golden moments shine again! REMEMBER THE GOOD TIMES!

5) Have faith in what you are selling, just as you believe that you yourself are top of the line—or find another job! BELIEVE, OR RECANT!

Now, what about that customer over there?

CHAPTER TWO
Fire-Starters

No one can succeed by playing the same way for each crowd.
—Yo Yo Ma

Fire-Starters

Barge in, throw out the glad hand, roll into your spiel full speed and then toss the order book into the customer's lap—that's real power selling, right?

Actually, that's the prescription for power failure, if not for power ridicule. Most successful salespeople would probably agree that the most prevalent misconception about selling is that the salesperson should be glib, voluble, overwhelming. Or, to say it straight out: a fast-talking con artist. The type of guy that, in old movies, could fleece a whole town full of hicks. But have you seen all that many wide-eyed rustics in your showroom lately?

No, you don't build trust by bowling over the customer with a pitiless barrage. If you become a windbag, you will blow your opportunities right out the door.

It's not power to overpower.

That's the first thing to remember before devising your strategy of exciting the customer. Real power doesn't show off, doesn't have to set off verbal fireworks. Real power is strength in reserve, held back until the proper moment.

In actual sales practice, that means you don't drown your sales prospect with talk. You are a human being, not a ventriloquist's dummy. The key in today's market is to seem to discuss a problem, not make a pitch. You and the customer are going to co-operate in making the sale. The goal is to reach agreement that the product or

34

service is a good thing—no, a necessary thing—for the customer to have. You want to light a fire, not perpetrate arson.

Let's try a step-by-step process. First of all, you have to clear away the deadwood and make room for that fire you mean to start.

FIRE-STARTER 1

Here's our first Fire-Starter:

Prepare the ground!

Does the customer have misconceptions about you and your product? Probably. Is there suspicion in the air, because of bad experiences with salespeople in the past, or disappointments with similar services? Maybe. It's up to you to clear the hearth so that you are in the controlling position.

Do you want to counteract the expectation that you'll come on too strong? Get the customer off guard (and win his respect) by projecting the opposite image. Do you want to get rid of the notion that, for example, your product is too costly? Immediately bring up the financial advantage of buying from you. Or bring up the argument you've designed to show that the extra cost is worth it.

In other words, your first step is to deal with that deadwood before it deals with you. You can't step over it, and you can't work around it. There's only one workable approach, from the angle of power selling: *Take whatever tactic is necessary to clear away all of the junked-up ideas and bad experiences that lie in the way.*

If you try to avoid such problems, they just get worse, in the customer's mind. He's sitting there, saying to himself something like, "Aha! This guy is trying to avoid talking about the way the flimjabber always falls off at three in the morning."

Maybe you don't always know what's in the way. Your prospect might have had a problem with your service or a similar one, but the problem might be so unusual that you can't be expected to anticipate it. So, keep your eyes and ears open, particularly the latter. As we'll be stressing time and again, one secret of interest*ing* talkers is that they are interest*ed* listeners.

Right off, you should zero in and discover whether or not your customer has some particular reason to be wary of you, your company or your product. Don't wince. Take a deep breath, and ask.

*Direct questions produce
straightforward answers, as a rule.*

Just look the prospect in the eye and ask, "Have you ever had trouble with our products?" or "Have you had any reason to complain about our service policy?" If the prospect has something to complain about, you have the opportunity to answer his complaint — a chance to show yourself as concerned about him as an individual and eager to back up your product or service. You have a chance to clear the obstructing deadwood.

And if he does *not* have a specific complaint, you've got him to agree that, yes, there's no reason to suspect the virtues of your product. When someone says, "No, I've never had any trouble with your inflatable ballpoint pen," you have a statement that you can build on. Or, to return to starting our fire, you have a choice bit of tinder.

FIRE-STARTER 2

That leads us to our second Fire-Starter:

Choose the right wood!

You wouldn't try wet bamboo for that romantic fire at the ski lodge, unless you wanted to make your companion think you're doing a Woody Allen imitation. A roaring fire takes the right ingredients—dry, aged wood. In the sales situation, you will have chosen your materials ahead of time. You will have answered the questions you anticipate: You'll be ready to present the good points and practiced at explaining or defending the weaker points. You'll know which arguments are distracting, rather than helpful. And you'll have found out which arguments *are* most helpful. You'll know, in short, what is available for you to use and what should be avoided.

But don't use any of it! Not, that is, until you begin working *with* the prospect. The idea is that you and he will build this fire together.

Pile on everything you have at your disposal, and you will probably have a confusing jumble, a great mixed-up pile. Why bring up a fault, for example, that the prospect himself has not considered? Why initiate a discussion of maintenance, when the prospect is only interested, or chiefly interested, in style or cost or availability? Why go into technical details when your prospect doesn't understand or care about how a product works?

Remember, be prepared to answer every question, but answer *only* those questions that interest the prospect.

How will you know which ones are important? By recalling the underlying theme of this chapter: **A secret of interest*ing* talkers is that they are interest*ed* listeners.** Listen to what your prospect says (which implies that you encourage him continually to talk). Then do better than that—listen *beneath* what he is saying. What is his unexpressed concern? Meanwhile, be watching. Let body language reveal his inner thoughts. Don't let the merest flicker of an expression escape your notice.

FIRE-STARTER 3

Good listening and close watching are your tools for responding to our third Fire-Starter:

Build that fire as a team!

How does that work? By putting on the logs that your customer, without knowing it, has just selected. You get a good fire going by piquing interest and letting it peak!

Suppose your prospect wants a car that reeks of gentrification. You leap on those features that suggest class, good taste, tradition. To put it in street language: Find where he's at, and meet him there.

As each log goes on the fire, the customer should feel the increasing heat of having his own needs satisfied. In fact, he should feel as if the product could only be described in the way that he understands. In other words, don't let him feel that he should be asking about rust-proofing if he's the kind of person who doesn't give a damn about rust-proofing. The two of you are working together to build a picture that will satisfy you both: **He has his questions, you have your answers—the choices are made mutually.**

All the time, you are watching to see whether his breath is getting a little shorter. Have you got him interested? That's not quite the right way to phrase it. The real question is: Have you helped him clarify the interest he already has? (Remember what we learned about customer commitment in Chapter One.) Is he becoming more excited, more deeply persuaded, because you have responded to his real needs? Well, he should be, if you have identified his interests and have been able to match your information to his profile.

Fire-Starters

Warning: Don't ruin good advice by clumsy handling. Responding to a customer, like responding to a friend or lover, is not a matter of vaulting into his arms at the first flicker of interest. There is a line invisibly drawn between salesperson and customer. Your aim is to bring the prospect closer to that line, even as you approach from the other side. You are to meet in the centre, not race across the line and drag the customer screaming to the finish.

In other words, you must not be over-eager when you are stacking up the wood for your fire. Don't pretend that you spend every night at the opera, just because your customer has his radio tuned to a classical music station. You know that, of course. But you should also remember that you don't make a sale by pretending that a Jeep is an amphibious vehicle or that a maroon plaid sports jacket will make your customer the envy of all the guests at a formal wedding.

You play to the customer's needs, but you don't go overboard in suggesting that your product was designed with him alone in mind. Your product can't do everything, and it probably won't be perfection in answering a customer's needs and desires, except in the rarest cases. Your prospect, unless he is a special kind of fool, doesn't expect your product to be perfection; he won't believe or respect your efforts to argue that it is. (And if he *is* that kind of fool, he's already been parted from his money, so you're wasting your time.)

So, be creative, but don't be offensive. Have the grace and good sense to back off when the customer comes up with a weakness in your product that, from his point of view, is important. Of course, as we suggested earlier, you were trying to avoid his bringing up the subject on his own terms by bringing it up yourself in the beginning.

But you can't always anticipate. When the customer's comment comes out of left field, you have to be quick on your feet. *But don't overdo it!* The heat may be building, but the fire is not lit; you'll botch the whole enterprise if you promise what obviously cannot be delivered. And, as we hope you already realize, you'll be insulting the customer. Respect is the mainspring of your mutual enterprise; it works both ways.

FIRE-STARTER 4

Now, with all the wood stacked up just right, it's time to set the whole thing alight!

Move on the beat!

Now, we're not leaving you on your own at this point, but we are suggesting that *only you* will know when to strike that match. It takes practice, like any art. It takes talent. It takes a gift for timing. Scared? no reason to be. Challenged? Every reason to be.

What does David Thomas, Dean of Cornell's School of Business, have to say about success in the field? "I think that Number One is the ability to handle uncertainty." Or what novelist Ernest Hemingway, that great chronicler of those who face danger, called "grace under pressure."

Cool. If you don't have it, you have to aim for it. Most of us don't have it. Successful sales personnel learn to imitate it, and then one day, they actually have it. (It's the old story of the Happy Hypocrite, the man who was really cruel and selfish but plastered a genial smile on his face each day until, when he died, the expression had taken over and he had actually become genial.)

But, cool or nervous, you are the one who has to decide exactly what will finally set your customer alight. If you move too soon, your efforts might go up in smoke. The materials weren't right, or they hadn't been properly set up. If you move too late, there will be too much wood piled up, and your little match won't be capable of setting off a conflagration. And then there's the question of the wind being right. . .

What's the answer? Practice. What's a better answer? Practice, practice.

And yet, the "gift" of knowing when to strike can be strengthened in some basic ways. Just as the old folk saying has it that genius is one percent inspiration and ninety-nine percent perspiration, it is true that sales "instinct" can be developed. *Fundamental to power selling is the concept of building upon your personal strengths, of trusting them as the foundation of your career.* So, when you are dealing with a prospect, remember what techniques have worked for you in bringing the other "deals" in your life to a climax.

How did you get the family car for a teenage date, or how did you persuade your five-year-old to walk alone into a new kindergarten class? How did you convince an employer to give you a break, and how did you cajole your spouse into going to the beach rather than the mountains for the last vacation?

Choose your own examples, then look closely at how you *operated*. Does that sound like a harsh word? Not at all. You wanted to bring someone you loved into agreement with an idea because you believed in the idea. You mounted a campaign, although you might not have considered it in that light.

Well, you should consider your relationship with your sales prospect in a similarly personal light. The two of you might be perfect strangers, but we've agreed that you are working *together* to make a sale; now, consciously or not, you must take advantage of your own personal style to decide when to set the customer you've brought to the burning point alight.

Be honest. Is it your smile, or your argumentative technique? Is it the way you tell a joke (be careful!), or is it the way you appeal to the other person's self-interest? By now, you should know what is most appealing in your own personality.

More important, you should be able to tell when you've reached your optimum of influence. When did Dad fork over the keys? Think about that moment, and aim for it. Don't wait for the customer to beg for a chance to buy, and don't rush in because you're afraid that he'll never be as warm as you want. He's a person.

The people you've been successful with in your personal life are persons, too. What works with them will work with the prospect. Trust your past record. (And if you want to call that "instinct," that's okay, too.)

Moving on the beat, to repeat our phrase, means to **move on the beat that is natural to you.** No one else hears your own beat. You do. It's where your power as a unique personality really lies.

SIT BACK A MOMENT

Has this chapter made you want to step right out and prove yourself with a new customer? If it has, then you're not likely to have severe problems in your career. It means you want to play the game. Just hearing about a sale has made you want to *be there*.

If you're on an aeroplane or train, why not turn to the person nearest you and see if there isn't an opportunity there? Why not? Don't you miss your work when you're forced to waste time? As a racing-car driver Mario Andretti has said, "There's nothing in the world that keeps you going more than pure enjoyment of your work." Centre upon somebody right now, if it makes sense to do so, and keep the ideas of this chapter in your mind. See for yourself how they work in action.

Here's a checklist of the ways to fire up a customer:

1) PREPARE THE GROUND!
2) CHOOSE THE RIGHT WOOD!
3) BUILD THAT FIRE AS A TEAM!

4) MOVE ON THE BEAT!

Checklists are a good aid to memory. In the next chapter, we'll be talking about six of the "Don't Forget/Don't Neglect" considerations that any salesperson should keep in mind for the life of a career.

CHAPTER THREE
Cardinal Dos and Cardinal Don'ts

I'm a chronically dissatisfied perfectionist.

—Rex Harrison

Cardinal Dos and Cardinal Don'ts

Today, not many people like to believe that there are ironbound, hard-and-fast rules for either personal or business behaviour. We all put a high price on individuality, and that's been a good thing for business and for the country. It's the individual approach, the individual commitment to achievement, that has typically been the bottom line of extraordinary achievement in America.

Nonetheless, pros in selling agree that there are certain Cardinal Dos and certain Cardinal Don'ts.

Now, you may be the kind of person who works best by proving the exception to the rule. And that's great, if it's really the power source of your selling style! But it's a good rule that it's best to know a rule before you break it—besides, we believe that the fundamental Dos and Don'ts of power selling are pretty much standard and trustworthy, upwards of ninety-nine percent of the time.

CARDINAL DO 1

The first cardinal rule is that you must:

Know it backwards!

And frontwards, too, of course. You should be as primed before a sale as a contestant on a television game show. Sure, you know the points you want to make, *if* you get to make them in your own good time. But what if the prospect interrupts, or wanders from the point, or heads for the jugular? You have to be prepared with facts, and then you have to work in light of the hidden *structure* of your argument.

Your pitch has a shape, doesn't it? Like a story, or a sure-fire joke, or (if you will) an alibi that holds up to cross-examination. When your prospect deflects you from the structure of your presentation, you have to edge him back. *You have to control the shape of the sales pitch.*

When you are in top form, it will look to your customer as if you're talking casually in a free-wheeling conversation, but a clever sales professional will recognize that, subtly and easily, you've geared the interchange to fit *your* structure.

CARDINAL DO 2

At least, where your competition is concerned:

See no evil!

That's right—it's a big mistake to start shortchanging another product or service. (If the prospect wants to do so, that's fine; listen wisely, then ease his complaint with your superior offer!)

First, any comparison can be a two-edged sword. Your product may be less expensive, but does it last as long, and so forth?

Second, someone who's bought a lemon is not unlike a spouse criticizing a spouse. One can say some pretty rough things, but if the other agrees, watch out! The owner of a lemon may enjoy grousing, but if you join the criticism of the product, he may think that you're calling him a fool.

Third, criticism of the competition brings an unpleasant tone to the sales conversation. You want to establish a friendly, reasonable atmosphere, a pleasant mood for discussing a fairly important decision. No one looks good with a sneer on his face. People seem less trustworthy when they disparage others.

Common sense, right? You don't want negatives in the air; you don't want your customer dredging up his own unfortunate experiences, because the overflow of such bad feelings will wash over you and the relationship you're trying to establish.

So, emphasize the good points of your product. See only the good. Sell only the good. It's a waste of time, or worse, to try to *un*sell the competition.

CARDINAL DO 3

There's no better way to say it:

Mind your manners!

We understand that you will often be nervous, as we've mentioned, and it may sometimes seem that the month's rent, or the holiday in Spain—or your whole career—will hinge upon one important sale. That's a problem. But it's not the customer's problem.

You may be a guest in a prospect's office or home,

but you must establish yourself as a kind of host. You are welcoming another person into your presentation. You've extended an invitation; you want him to be comfortable; you will be hospitable. On a sales floor, of course, this attitude is even more critical, because the potential customer might be unnerved or unsure and be all too conscious of the direction and distance of the nearest exit.

If necessary (and in today's changing society, it *is* necessary for many of us), don a mask, sneak over to a bookstore and, yes, buy a standard book of etiquette.

Also, learn to be aware of the social mores of your own territory. You may be surprised that you've missed the obvious. You might insult a woman in a big city, say, by assuming that she is married, and vice versa in a small town elsewhere. **Assumptions are always dangerous.** You don't want to suggest that a woman ask her son's opinion, as he stands there, and discover that the man's her boyfriend.

Any assumption you make is an invasion of privacy— whether it's the comparatively innocent assumption that a prospect regularly watches television, or goes to church, or likes to golf. These are all, if you think about it, loaded with danger.

One other thing: **Watch your language.** Not just the hard stuff, but simple terms that trip you up. In a certain area of the country, in a certain social class, you'll be thought a fool if you say "home" rather than "house," "toilet" rather than "loo".

Do you care? You'd better. Someone ready to lay

down several thousand pounds to carpet her drawing room may not be happy to deal with someone who is so *déclassé* as to call it her lounge.

Reverse snobbery or right-on-the-button snobbery, the clever salesperson learns to recognize the trends and catch the next wave. Soon, you'll be able to afford a house with any number of rooms and call them what you want!

CARDINAL DO 4

The next rule is: **Be honest . . .
sensibly!**

Let's not get cynical about this; if there's the appropriate surge of power in your sales presentation, you're not going to have to weasel around the truth about your product. The force of your honesty about its good qualities should carry the day.

On the other hand, flattery and so-called "polite lies" are the grease that keeps society running smoothly. You don't have to tell a lady of a certain age that a new dress will take years off her figure, but you can honestly react to the improvement a tasteful dress might bring. You may suspect that a harried businessman who decides to buy an expensive electric organ is really not going to get much actual use out of it, but that's not your decision. **In other words, you have a responsibility to help the customer buy what he wants to buy —not what you feel he should buy.**

Yes, there's a thin line. If he or she is asking for your

help in making a tasteful decision, you should be diplomatic but straight. If a couple wants to furnish their English Tudor house with orange futons and tables made of Plexiglas, let them—but woe betide the salesperson who convinces them to make such a choice even if they have no strong feelings about it. You can't depend upon their friends and relatives to be quite so lacking in good sense. You won't like the reverberations.

CARDINAL DO 5

Make a friend for life!

Well, "friend" may be too strong a word, in the sense of exchanging gifts at Christmas or going out together to paint the town, but the powerful sale should cement a long-lasting relationship. The satisfied customer, like the satisfied patient, is the best advertisement you have available.

As F. James McDonald, president of the General Motors Corporation, has said, "I don't believe that advertising ever gets you a quality reputation. If you don't have it, advertising won't help you a bit. And if you do have it, word of mouth is enough."

Your surest asset—the foundation of your base of power as a successful salesperson—will be your reputation. Satisfied customers return; they spread the word about the good experience they had with you.

You want a customer's friends to walk up to his new purchase and envy it. You want them to be astonished that you were able to convince him to buy something so sensible rather than be amused or horrified at what you got away with.

Some top sales personnel send birthday cards to their customers, or congratulatory notes when a wedding or birth in the family is announced. These gestures work if they don't look contrived, but you will find your own ways to make a customer a friend.

CARDINAL DON'T 1

Now for the negatives. We've also set down five important Don'ts, and maybe they're not all so obvious from the commonsense standpoint. Let's see. The first is:

Don't accept defeat!

What's that word? **Defeat?** We haven't mentioned any such thing in *this* book! But there might come a day when you let it creep unnoticed into your vocabulary, and there it will grow and grow, eating away at your strength and vigour as a salesperson.

Now, as we've suggested, the power approach to selling does not imply that you wrestle your unwilling prospect to the floor. But inner power will make you stubborn in pursuit. **What you have to distinguish, though, is defeat at the hands of one person from defeat in general.** In other words, sometimes you will want to return again and again to a prospect. At other times, you will want to continue to search for new prospects.

In either case, whichever is appropriate, you have not admitted defeat; you have defined the problem. Either a prospect needs further nurturing, which means that your first meeting was the first step in a process (rather than a once-and-final encounter), or you need to find different prospects, in which case the sales encounter that looks like defeat was actually a kind of winnowing: You learned what type of person needs your product, what type of problem it best answers.

You seize the power to redefine the encounter that a less competent salesperson might write off as defeat. *It is never defeat.* It is always something else, if you invest your resources in rethinking the event.

CARDINAL DON'T 2

What about your colleagues in the business?

Don't ignore the person beside you!

Sure, there's competition, and it's healthy to want to be better than everyone else in your league. *But don't forget that the other men and women who sell are your finest and most accessible resources.* Swap stories of your best days, and your worst. Ask for advice—and don't be shy about giving it. Just like a sports star, you're on your own when you meet the prospect, but you need the support and knowledge of the rest of the team when you come off the field.

A salesperson can see you in action; this book can't.

Cardinal Dos and Cardinal Don'ts

A salesperson who really loves his work as you should will be happy to share with you. Helping you reach your full power potential will not threaten him—in fact, it's the other way around. *When you get better, he gets better.* One powerhouse working in a vacuum is a lifeless enterprise. Two powerhouses reacting off each other throwing off sparks—now, there's potential for excitement! Just be sure to choose the salespeople who face the day with eagerness, who count the challenges rather than the hours of the day. And who respect their customers.

CARDINAL DON'T 3

This respect leads us to the third Don't:

Don't put customers in the zoo!

You've seen the kind of salesperson who gets a kick out of ridiculing his customers. The "here-come-the-animals" approach. Well, if you think you're in sales to toss peanuts at dumb primates, you're on the road to unhappiness. You might get a few cheap laughs along the way, but you'll be belittling your own potential for success while you're belittling the very people who should be your partners in the sales process.

No, they're not animals—even if they rush on the floor in crowds, or remain ignorant about the mechanics of the car they want to buy, or have put on their most expensive designer dress upside down.

Come on! Who are you to assert some sort of un-earned superiority, just because you know the turf? Some of these very people could waltz around you on *their* home turf. Most of them are decent, if not over-whelmingly successful or imposing. And all of them are there because, deep down, they need you, and they trust you. It's a stupid betrayal of trust to dismiss your prospects as fools to be conned.

As we've said, **power must be transmitted back and forth between salesperson and prospect.** The relationship must be based upon respect. When you're tired or angry, you might want to make a crack about someone who has just proved difficult. Don't. It's the first step towards developing an automatic contempt, towards blaming the prospects when you don't make a sale.

Remember: You must never catch yourself thinking that only a fool would walk away from your presenta-tion. Your power in sales will come from the conviction that a wise man was, for some reason outside your con-trol, unable to hear you properly.

You didn't fail, but you *were* distracted from the proper course. *Back to it!*

With the next prospect you will zoom in on his best points, bring them out, and come to a personal under-standing—if not always to a sale. (After all, and it's time to say it aloud, sometimes you will do the prospect and yourself the service of discovering that the product is simply not necessary, or desirable.) Don't disparage the customer!

CARDINAL DON'T 4

Yes, you can be charming, but:

Don't be shy about your motives!

Discussing football teams is fine, but it's secondary to the goal. Don't fall into the trap of letting your prospect forget that he's there to do business. You want to make a sale!

Sound obvious? You may be surprised at how frequently the sales conversation trails off into chitchat. **Don't forget your basic aim.** Charm is the tool, casual conversation the instrument.

Hypocrisy? If you think that, then our message has not been getting through. You want to take those individual resources we've talked about, the power to which only you have direct access, and burn brightly for your customer.

But don't let stardom go to your head. You've still got to pay the backstage crew. Your talents are concentrated upon the sale, and the customer knows that. Both of you know that the process has to be relaxed from time to time—that you can't build up a head of steam without taking a moment's rest occasionally.

But the aim is the sale. Negotiation is meant as a path to agreement. Don't confuse the means with the end: You can impress people; you can entertain them. But Job One, as the expression goes, is to get their names on a dotted line.

CARDINAL DON'T 5

You've got the prospect right alongside you, focusing, looking for the best angle, ready to shoot.

Don't miss the click of the shutter!

Be sure you're ready to click that shutter, to take the picture at the *exact* moment that he is. No, it's not easy, and maybe you don't really have to be that precise about judging the moment. *But that should be your aim.*

And don't be afraid of running out of film. If you bring him to focus, and he gets past you, start in again. **You can't get a commission from a sale you don't clinch—and timing is everything.** Whole books are written about just this moment, the closing of the sale. (In fact, a whole section of this book has been devoted to closing the sale.)

Pick your own image—strike while the iron is hot (if you like), or fire when you see the whites of their eyes! You have to be alert, ready, eager—and primed!

As tennis player Jimmy Connors says, "I give everything I've got every time I go out there, and I'm proud of that." *With that attitude you can't lose. You might not make every sale, but you're never a loser.*

And it helps to look back on these ten hints to power selling from time to time. They hook you into the *best* that you can do.

AFTERWORD

Afterword

This first section is an introduction to the basics. It's short, but it's intense. You'll want to re-read it after your next day of selling and see whether or not certain ideas here have come to life in a new and vital way for you.

From yourself, however, has to come the enthusiasm that fuels the power. You have to decide that your work is not a form of imprisonment but in fact an opportunity for the liberation of all the talent and personality that lie within you. You have to get up in the morning feeling like octogenarian George Burns: "I can't get old—I'm working. I was old when I was 21 and out of work. As long as you're working you stay young."

You're going to save yourself a lot of stress if you can adopt that attitude. You're going to make sales, and you're going to amaze people who wonder where your sense of joy comes from. Because if you look around, you're not going to find all that many people who really enjoy their work. You can, and you will—if you recognize that sales can be for you the release and expression of all that is best in you.

***Sales can be your ticket to power
living.***

PART TWO: COLD CALLS, HOT LEADS AND POWER PROSPECTING

INTRODUCTION TO PART TWO

Introduction to Part Two

This book is designed to help you develop your sales potential to its fullest—to help you identify and maximize the talents and strengths unique to you.

But all your efforts will be wasted—and lead to frustration and the danger of self-doubt—*if* you're all fired up and have no target! Energy has to find the proper outlet. A full head of steam can move a mountain—blow the whole business to smithereens—or just fizzle in the empty air.

You, like every other sales professional committed to success in the marketplace, have to master the raw energies you build within yourself. You have to take clear-sighted, steady aim; you have to know what *you* want.

Your goals should be specific, not vague and dreamy.

The dreamer says, "I want to be rich. I want to be powerful. I want to build." The dreamer isn't saying anything useful; he's just dreaming.

The visionary (and that's *you*) says, "I want an income of £250,000 a year by 1995. I want to be regional vice-president in charge of retail sales. I want to open 10 new dealerships within a 100-mile radius over the next 15 years." Now, that's visionary—but it's not dreamlike. It's specific. It takes aim.

It also puts you to the test: When you don't reach a specific goal within a specific period of time, you're keeping the pressure on. . .you can't blink and look the other way. . .you can't escape into vague ideas of imaginary progress.

> *A specific goal is also a specific*
> *benchmark*
> *of success.*

It's tougher to be a visionary than a dreamer. Centring on a goal takes time, and it takes thought. It takes a realistic—but optimistic—appraisal of the power you bring to the sales process.

It also takes a kind of, well, lust—what New York Senator Daniel Moynihan has called "the primordial capitalist urge." You seek out your goal as vigorously as the caveman lunges after his mate. Says Moynihan: "The great corporations of this country were not founded by ordinary people. They were founded by people with extraordinary energy, intelligence, ambition, aggressiveness. All those factors go into the primordial capitalist urge."

Yes, that's awesome power—energy, intelligence, ambition, aggressiveness. But the urge has an *object.* You have to take aim. And before you reach your long-range goals, there is the reality of the present. You've got the primordial capitalist urge, but who's listening? Who cares? Where's the action?

> *In other words:*
> *where's the prospect?*

Introduction to Part Two

Chances are, no matter how grand your ambitions in sales, your dead-eye aim is too often wasted on a vast and empty horizon. *Where's the target? How do you get the prospects you need? Do you just sit back and wait for something to swim by the reef?* Not if you want to work to capacity, you don't!

You have to prospect for prospects, unless you're in a very unusual sales situation. You have to find people who have never heard of you, and may never have heard of your product or service. You have to contact people who think they don't want to be contacted, and show them they're mistaken. You have to start early and keep going after others have packed it in for the day. You have to believe that you can find prospects in unlikely places—

But wait. It's not a matter of blind faith and cockeyed optimism.

> *It's Power Prospecting—an attitude,*
> *a way of thinking, a practical*
> *approach that has worked for top-*
> *flight personnel across the*
> *country—but it's also a plan*
> *of action.*

There are guidelines—even rules, if you will. There are no-no's. There are some grey areas, frankly, where you will be left to your own ingenuity. (And isn't that the best part—proving to yourself that you're the one who's got it?)

In Part Two:

- You'll learn to avoid the failure of passivity, which has blighted many a sales career.
- You'll learn to find prospects—not wait shyly for them to arrive.
- You'll learn how to keep them, when you find them.
- You'll learn how to develop a powerful network of sales contacts that will become the power base of your career in sales.

In short, you will learn all about Power Prospecting.

CHAPTER ONE
How Do You Get To Know
Who You Need To Know?
(Whiner's Excuse A: "It's all in who
you know.")

It's All in Who You Know

Okay, you think you're a tough-minded realist. You look around at successful people, and you say, "They all know somebody; that's how the world goes around."

You think you see politicians reaching high office because of *who they know*, or starlets getting choice parts—*who they know*. And you think to yourself (well, not you, but the passive, negative you that surfaces in all of us when we're feeling weak) you think, "Well, I don't know anybody."

Is it all in who you know?

Of course it is!

But that's no reason to give up. On the contrary, it's the key. Remember: The people who *know* people had to *meet* people. And so can you!

Think about it. Oh, sure, a very tiny proportion of the population is born "knowing" people. You can envy them, if you like, but that only breeds negative feelings; that's a game plan for failure. You can start a revolution if you like, but that's probably going to take a lot of time and energy. (And *we* thought you wanted to make a high-level career in sales!)

Besides, that tiny proportion born "knowing" people aren't your competition. They know the ones they know, but they don't know everybody. Your real competition comes from the 99 + % of the business world that *learns* to know people.

And your real opportunity comes from the 99 + % of the people—not born "knowing everybody," either—who are themselves waiting to be known.

> *If you don't know them,*
> *Power Prospecting puts it a slightly*
> *different way: You just don't*
> *know them yet.*

To *know* people you have to *meet* them; that's the theme of this chapter, because, at the bottom line, success really is related to who you know—and who knows you!

NETWORKING FOR NEW BUSINESS

Buoy yourself up with a nonpolitical political example. The two most powerful leaders in our world got where they are, in part, because they knew people. But neither Ronald Reagan nor Mikhail Gorbachev, born in obscure parts of their respective countries, was born to influence. They won it, whatever you think of them as individuals. They met, and they met, and they met . . .

And they pursued a course something like this:

Take Stock

That's right. Square one. Who *do* you know? That's the power base you have to define.

It might be the customers you've already serviced—and satisfied. Did you let them just walk out the door? Do you keep files? Do you give them a personal business card, so they can tell their relatives and friends about you?

We're not talking about resources based upon years of sales effort.

It's All in Who You Know

Once you have made your very first
sale, you have begun to build your
Sales Power Base.

You've not only made a sale; you've also got the potential for a ripple effect throughout the community—or,
even better, throughout that customer's network of
business or personal contacts.

The first sale is the beginning of being known. A satisfied customer is power potential—*if* you take control
of the "power" controls. The customer is not just an
individual; he or she is your introduction, if you take
advantage of the opportunity, to scores, or hundreds, or
even *thousands* of prospects.

And if you're in sales and have a track record of many
satisfied customers—well, your potential for worthwhile sales prospects is well-nigh unlimited. Just count
'em up.

Think of it this way: Each sale can kindle other sales.
One sale can have explosive force—and it's up to you to
harness the potential release of energy.

How so? Well, as we've already suggested by impli-
cation, you should get the dogtags on everyone you sell
to—and everyone who hasn't been convinced (*yet*).
View each sales effort as the tip of the iceberg—the $\frac{7}{8}$
not showing gives you opportunity, even if you have to
dive for it.

Don't write anyone off; write them down—name, telephone number, address, profile. What you do with this information will depend upon your business. If you sell big-ticket items, you might want to call your customers every six months or so, and ask if they're satisfied. That makes your annual call sound more natural, when you suggest that the newer model is worth thinking about.

If you're working retail in a department store, you might want to send a personal note—or just a postcard—before a big sale. If you're on the road, it doesn't hurt to send a client a news clipping about a local outlet of his company, or a brief congratulatory note about the firm's rise on the stock market. You know your business, so you'll know what pleases your customer—and what reminds him of the service you have given, and can give again.

The point is: **Don't let the customer get away, even** *after* **you've made a sale.** Hold on to him. He's your capital investment in the growth of your pool of prospects.

The Ripple Effect

Now you have to get the reverberations from those sales you've made. You have to maximize the ripple each successful sale can make in the prospect pool.

That process begins when you simply continue a casual, but steady, business relationship with your customers. The family will notice the personal notes, the concerned telephone calls. Even in this era of the nuclear family, the word will get to Aunt Jean or Cousin Bill that here's a salesperson who is unusually caring and on top of the game—in other words, unusually competent!

And who do people trust most? The guy who makes millions, or the guy who comes on strong, or the guy who obviously enjoys his work, and has pride in achieving? Of course, we all tend to trust the person who derives satisfaction from his job—after all, satisfying us is what gives *him* satisfaction. That's how it works in sales. And just consider the image you can create with people you wouldn't otherwise meet, if you establish regular contacts with every customer you sell to.

You'll be amazed at how many people suddenly know you—and want some of the same treatment themselves.

You'll soon be amazed at who you know!

Warning: Success in gaining prospects depends upon projecting the right image, at full incandescent power. You don't just hold a customer's hand; you remain prepared to deliver!

Let's say your big-ticket item—as can happen to the best of us—may not be all it's cracked up to be. Anyway, that's what you're told when you make your call. By the bones of all sainted successful sales personnel, *do not chicken out!* You take a risk in those calls, and you have to be ready to take the consequences. It won't always be plain sailing.

Face the music: Whether it's a free service call, or some additional rebate—whatever can be reasonably offered and is appropriate for restoring your product's credibility—make sure you do something, even if you have to subsidize it!

By exposing yourself, spreading the word that you are the concerned professional, you are also at risk, frankly. (And do we have to tell you which travels the faster and the more effectively—good news or bad, praise or condemnation?)

Big winnings are the reward of big risks—so make sure you recognize the stakes. **The power in your advance upon potential prospects must never be turned back against you;** there's no money to be made these days in falling upon your own sword. In other words: Be prepared to answer complaints. Do so promptly. Do so cheerfully. There may be a short-term loss, but the phones will be buzzing: "This bloke actually got it fixed *for nothing!*" It's stories like that—well, they're the real thing. They'll bring new customers on the run.

The Tidal Wave Effect

Not satisfied with word of mouth?

Good. We aren't, either. Power Prospecting requires extra effort, heightened imagination. Go back to what you've put down on paper about each customer and consider that important fourth item: The Profile.

It's All in Who You Know

Now, look for similarities between the characteristics of that profile and the ideal profile of a customer for your product or service.

Say that your customer belongs to the country club, and you sell golfing equipment. You know how to handle that one. But the same reasoning can work on less obvious levels.

A regular customer is active in her church, so you offer discounts for the altar flowers (while recalling the cardinal rule of never discussing religious beliefs or political convictions!). . .or you know one of your clients loves to be part of his son's football club, so you get the boss to sponsor some uniforms . . . or a customer who regularly buys dresses belongs to a luncheon club, and you arrange for a visiting makeup expert to make a guest appearance to discuss beauty secrets.

What these ideas have in common is a power shift—from just one customer to the customer's peer group. Through him, you and your product become familiar—become *known*—to many more people like him. His friends become your friends, because you've shown that you know how to be a friend.

There's the beauty of hands-on contact here. Your original contact or sale was your opportunity to prove your worth; each step after that benefits from the first person-to-person encounter. Your influence will spread in a physical way, a dynamic relationship growing at a *geometric* rate.

*In short order, you'll know
who you need to know!*

And, much better off than the tiny majority born "knowing" people, you'll not be wasting your time getting to know people who won't be useful to you. **Power Prospecting is target orientated.** You'll choose where to make friends. Who you know will be who you decide to know. The focus will be yours, not the result of chance.

Star Time?

It's a media age, but don't count on advertising or public-relations techniques to make friends for you.

Exposure can give you or your company name recognition. Rarely, and we mean *rarely*, is an individual gifted with that mysterious quality that glows on camera or in print photos.

But don't bet on it.

Don't expect your ad manager or your layout artists to do your work for you. *Advertising doesn't necessarily produce prospects; it will, at best, get the current flowing around the reef and the fish will swim by in shoals.*

But who are they? What do they want? How can they be persuaded to consider your product—and buy?

Only you can answer those questions. You're the expert. You're the one who knows—or is learning—how to build upon your power base of successful sales and bring in prospects with strong sales potential for you. Don't let the video glitter blind you; don't lose faith in your own resources and expect to ride piggy-back off the advertising campaigns.

In the final analysis, what matters is the spark ignited between you and the customer. And it's more likely to flare up when you have Power Prospected yourself into contact with exactly the right people—the new friends you've made as outlined in this chapter.

Who you know is up to you!

CHAPTER TWO
Cultivating Contacts
(Whiner's Excuse B: "They're just friends of friends; they really didn't want to buy.")

Cultivating Contacts

So you've made the contacts, but they just want to be pals? You gave their school orchestra a discount, so all they want to talk about is Sousa marches? You gave Uncle Charles a great deal on a truck, so all they want is advice on how to sue the guy who sold them a used estate that turns the highways red with flaking rust?

Hey, don't forget that *you're* the one who knows where the power lies. You're the one who likes the challenge—and challenge it most definitely is—of moving your prospect from acquaintance to customer . . . from chit-chat to profitable, goal-oriented business discussion.

It takes class.

Not snobbery, or showing off, or some kind of pseudo-yuppie gloss and shine. The "class" we mean comes from confidence plus competence—belief in your own skills.

It takes sincerity.

The real kind, not the prepackaged, freeze-dried, add-a-little-water kind. You have a legitimate aim; it can be dovetailed with your prospect's legitimate aims. The prospect knows that you sell for a living. This is not a dirty little secret to be avoided in polite conversation. You know that the prospect—if your focus in Power Prospecting has been clear—is a potential customer.

That's not a dirty little secret, either.

It takes brain power. In your job, you have to work on all burners. Successful sales work is not for the lazy! When you face a prospect, you have to be **on,** just like a lounge comic or a president at a press conference (though with a somewhat different style, of course). You have to be thinking about the prospect's profile. How does he know you, or know of you? What does he expect from you? What does he assume about your tastes or ideas, because of the nature of his connection with you? What do you want to build on? Are there any land mines? (Maybe he's just divorced the wife whose brother thinks you're Santa Claus, or maybe he thinks the toys your company donated to the Variety Club Christmas charity were pretty tasteless. Or maybe he's just the cautious type. Assume nothing.)

To get control of all the potential, take these steps:

1) Get Your Bearings

Tune into what's being said, and what's not being said.

Draw out the prospect, but don't let him wander. Chat about the mutual friend, or the mutual interest, and establish just exactly how much he knows about you. Find out the portrait in his mind so that you can fine-tune those areas where it might not precisely match the picture you want to present.

Find out what he wants—even if he doesn't think he knows (unconsciously, he does; we all do, all the time), or doesn't feel ready to tell you.

Just stopped by to talk? Not very likely. (But if it *is* true, you'll have to change his aim, or move him along politely. You're at work; you're on call; you're not there to entertain someone whose wife has been delayed at the office.)

You have to pick up on the clues available, or produce some. What's the thing he remembers most strongly? The "good idea" you gave someone, or the helpful explanation, or the card you sent when a grandson was born? Whatever it is, that's your clue to the customer: He wants more of the same. In a reverse way, it's your clue to what he hasn't been getting elsewhere.

So, discover why he's chosen you. We never see ourselves clearly, but in sales you have to try. It's even harder to see how others see us, as Robert Burns noted poetically a long time ago. But you've got to determine how your new prospect sees you, so you can take the ball from there.

Remember:

Only give what's asked for.

You may have ten of the most important qualities any salesperson could have—all on beck and call at your fingertips. But if this new prospect wants to be your friend, he's got one reason, or two. If he wants your honesty, you don't have to dazzle him with your technical expertise, and so on. *Give him what he came for, and save the rest for someone else.*

2) Action! Camera!

As in any sales encounter, you are the scriptwriter, and you should have it blocked out beforehand. Know your lines—but watch your audience. *The plot:* to convert the prospect you've found by Power Prospecting into a customer conspiring in the sales act.

You're the lead. Using your own judgement about timing, you bring up the subject of sales interest as soon as possible. Not so abruptly as to seem (and be) impolite, but in good time. There's no power in being an extra—you are not a fly on the wall in this production.

Say it again: You're the lead. If the prospect doesn't like this movie, he can walk out. He won't, though, if you take control. As we've said, he's there because he's interested in something he's heard you have. You've just figured out what that something is—so flaunt it!

Does he back off? Let him, for a few minutes. Why not show him a sports car like the one his cousin bought, just to keep the conversation on track? Or go to the rack and show how clever the prospect's friend was to choose the well-tailored or durable coat rather than another one.

In other words, ride the mutual friend's coat tails! Don't praise your work in the earlier sale; the prospect's heard it already. Praise the good sense of that mutual friend, planting the idea that the prospect can win similar respect from you, the professional, by making a similarly wise buying decision.

But don't tread water too long. Bring the prospect

back to the nitty gritty: Doesn't he want one, too?

If he still shies away, it's time to reap the benefits of his profile. (*Warning:* This advice is to be executed with tact and common sense, not with the blunt end of a meat-axe.) How does your service or product fit into that profile? Does he need a new suit for the Rotary Club's annual banquet? Camping equipment for the Legion's hike in a national park? Can your catering service give his daughter's wedding reception the kind of professional polish he enjoyed at a banquet honouring the mayor?

The danger, of course, is to seem to see a club or activity dear to your prospect in a purely venal light.

No danger if you don't feel that way. No danger, that is, if you don't have any unprocessed guilt feelings about transforming a personal contact into a sales encounter. . .

Cut: Let's pause and think this through. Is it morally wrong, or a little questionable, to mix business with friendship. . .to expect a gift to charity, say, to make our business known to potential customers. . .to send out holiday greetings to old customers, hoping that they will send friends your way?

We obviously don't think so—and we think you will agree that these examples, and many others, are a legitimate and socially useful method of making yourself and your services known to people who can benefit from them.

If you think that Power Prospecting is not entirely above board, maybe you've got some unresolved conflicts about sales work itself. Maybe you've listened to the cynics who think that the act of selling is by definition a rip-off, that products are always going to be shoddy and salespeople will always be sleazy . . . maybe you don't have the *pride* essential to being a good salesperson.

Yes, we mean it.

Power comes from pride.

From the decision to sell what you believe in. From the conviction that every reasonable customer is going to have reason to be grateful to you . . . and that your work in sales is important to society.

We believe that. We want you to. If you have a low self-esteem about selling, because you've listened to the cynics, work on it fast, before you waste a life—a career—making yourself miserable.

And if you *don't* have guilt feelings clogging your pathway, you should realize that there's everything to be gained—on both sides—by blending business with friendship, *so long as the rules are clear.*

3) Wrap It Up!

If the prospect isn't buying today, don't prolong the misery. He will appreciate knowing that you and he agree on the definition of your relationship.

If he's not buying, you're not selling.

Politely, let him know that you have to go back to work. There's no other prospect around? Well, let him know that it's not all on the surface, this profession of selling. Tell him that you've got to do some telephoning for leads, or have to study the new product manuals while the floor is quiet. Gently, let him understand that the time he gave you was part of your working day. In other words, let him know—without saying so—that you consider those few minutes an investment in the future.

Remind him why he came. Did Joe send him, or did he see your name as a sponsor of a community theater production? Get back to Square One so he'll remember the good feelings that brought him in and associate them with you in the flesh.

Also, if you end on a note of mutual interest, with a greeting for Joe or a compliment about the community theatre group, you've planted another useful seed: this prospect will be mentioning you to someone else again. You remain a part of the conversational landscape, and that's where you want to be.

Let the fat lady sing. It's not over, as you know, until she does, so give the prospect one last aria. New products are coming in next month: should you call? Prices may be dropping soon: would he like a notice sent to his office?

And don't hesitate to ask him to send his friends along. If he didn't buy, maybe he'll feel a twinge of guilt and make the effort to mention your name around. If he did buy, he'll want to show off, so remind him just how wise a purchase he made—and how good a deal you gave him.

Warning: Money may talk, but it *is* certainly talked about. If you're in the position to give special deals, don't go overboard with one customer and then expect his friends to be satisfied with less. For him, the deal is a pleasant surprise. Once the word's out, it's taken for granted—at least by that customer's circle of friends. You will have to have a good reason for making that exception: for example, the particular model is being discontinued by the factory. Otherwise the sweet deal will leave a sour taste all over town.

Never forget that word-of-mouth works both ways. Truly.

CHAPTER THREE
When the Tough Get Going
(Whiner's Excuse C: "I meet all the wrong people.")

When the Tough Get Going

Here's a truth it takes some people a lifetime to learn:

It's easier to meet the Chairman
than the Deputy Manager
of Stockroom and Supplies.

Maybe you've already learned that, and it's really no mystery: The man at the top has learned to organize his time. He doesn't have anything to prove, and he's ready to make decisions. He's in the position of being able to say yes or no.

Now, it's not always a good thing to "power sell" your way to the Chairman, because it's usually not necessary. But it *is* always sensible to find the source of power—and aim for it.

What that means depends upon what you sell.

If you sell expensive furniture in a town-centre store, you've got to reach your upper-middle-class target somehow. If you sell industrial equipment and can't get an appointment with the relevant buyer in a nationwide firm, you've got to break through somehow. If you are representing Russian ballet dancers who've just leapt over the Iron Curtain, you have to beat a path to the audiences that will appreciate them.

These things you *have to do* somehow (notice we don't append the phrase "or give up").

Let's talk about **Three Ways of Reaching the Unreachable:**

- Over the wall
- Down the Ladder
- Across the Table

Each is useful in specific situations only. Each requires a dash of courage, laced with humour, and a fund of common sense. And not everyone will be comfortable with all three of these approaches. There has to be a proper marriage of salesperson with approach—or disaster can result.

OVER THE WALL

You've met the impenetrable wall of polite rejection.

Everything is being handled by the book.

They will call you when they need you. They appreciate your interest. They wish you well. They hope you will call again. They regret that the buyer is otherwise occupied. They compliment your tie.

But they aren't buying!

Do you try the bulldog approach—just come back, again and again, watching the photos on the receptionist's desk reach adulthood, hoping that tenacity is rewarded? You could. We know salespeople who do. And they can always tell you about the one buyer who, after a quarter of a century, finally succumbed and took one order. One. Or maybe two.

Well, we didn't know you had that long. Power Prospecting isn't about digging up fossils. We thought you were charged up to play the game *on your own terms*—designed for the future you've laid out for yourself. Well, aren't you? Read on.

Tenacity is a fine thing. Ask any
Jack Russell. But it's passive,
when you get right down to it.

Stubbornness can get you somewhere sometimes, but it's more likely to keep you locked in place. To get moving, and keep moving in the right direction you've chosen, *you have to take a more creative approach.* You have to believe that all problems have answers—and that you can find the answer to the problem that seems to be blocking you.

Take that wall of politeness. In real life, if it were a real wall, you wouldn't hesitate, if there were a rich prize on the other side. You'd vault the thing. So why not leap?

The objective: the buyer who won't see you.

The method: whatever's appropriate.

Don't ignore the obvious. You are courting—*and you aim to please!* Find out from in-house newsletters, or the trades, or from office gossip, what the buyer enjoys in his spare time, for example. Let's say he loves to crochet. No, you don't send him an expensive gift of rare threads, but you might mail him an article you just happened to find outlining the therapeutic benefits of crocheting as a hobby for busy executives—and enclose a brief note with your card.

Does he know what you're up to? Of course, and he's likely to respect the effort. Do you pretend that you'd like to discuss exotic stitches sometime? No. He certainly wouldn't respect that lie. Will he simply ignore your thoughtful gesture? Not unless he doesn't deserve to be where he is—in which case, just wait; he won't be there long.

A personally targeted gesture of this sort gets a part of your personality past the receptionist. If

you've taken proper aim, based upon a clear under-
standing of your goals and your potential client's needs,
you should get a direct hit.

With that opening, as we've discussed elsewhere in
this book you'll be able to sound out the limits of your
potential in that sales situation.

DOWN THE LADDER

This is a risky approach, but it can be fun.

When you can't get satisfaction
at the lower levels, start at the top!

The possible pitfalls are many, of course. If you mis-
step, you can make implacable enemies on the lower
rungs of the corporate ladder. You can anger a higher-
up who will happily pass a complaint along to your
superiors. You can feel like a fool, and you can be un-
ceremoniously booted out on your behind.

But, when all else fails, wouldn't it be fun to try?

Business folklore is filled with tales of brave young
salespersons or inventors going to the top and reaching
the ear of the Chairman. Are they true? Sometimes,
probably.

**It doesn't matter whether or not a good myth is
true, but whether or not you and the top guy you're
after share a belief that it's true.** Even the most hardened executive likes a Cinderella story. Most successful
people are happy to see a beginner on the make; it reminds them of their own beginnings. Yes, if you make

it to the inner sanctum, you might get a fair hearing.

But there are two more pitfalls: style and competence.

Style: Most people say you either have it, or you don't. Not true. You *learn* it—let us never forget that Fred Astaire came from Nebraska and spent his formative years in vaudeville.

The style appropriate to dealing with a top executive depends upon many factors. It's not quite the same in the City as in Mayfair. But if you know your business, you know the style.

Yes, we're talking about a gamble. It's a last-ditch effort, when all else fails. But it just might work: Presidents *are* more accessible than vice-presidents.

But be wary of our second pitfall. If you're not prepared, you can really shoot yourself in the foot—and that's about the most painful of all wounds.

Competence: Have your story ready, and be able to deliver at machine-gun speed. The chief may deign to see you, if you've got his interest, and he may be grudgingly sympathetic to your efforts—but he doesn't have all day. He doesn't need you for a friend. He's willing to listen for five minutes—less if you babble, more if you've got something to say.

You've got to follow through.

It's admirable when the kid from the provinces battles her way into a Broadway audition and tries out for the starring role. It's a bore if she can't hit a note.

You should be ready to sing on key full voice—*every word packed with information.* You are a walking summary—as succinct as a memo, and just as businesslike.

Truth to tell, you can't make a habit out of bearding the lion in his den. But in the rare situations where that's the only way left to reach your prospect—go for it! You can turn disadvantage to advantage, a weak position into a powerful platform for future leverage.

It's a route for those who love a test—and expect to pass with flying colours.

ACROSS THE TABLE

You have to be good at this one, too. Back-slapping at the bar is not our idea of power in action. And if you believe that the apex of the art of business socializing is winning the heart and hand of the boss's daughter, we can only wish you Godspeed.

Most of us are going to try the social aspect of power selling in very conventional settings: restaurants, clubs, theatre lobbies, meetings of community groups.

And the problem in all of this is basic: Who's picking up the tab?

No, not just the bill for the food—although that can become a touchy issue, too. But it's the symbol of something more complex: **That is, in social situations, where do you draw the line of propriety?**

If you were a guest in a friend's house, would you abuse his hospitality when you get another guest off in a corner and bend his ear about refrigerator parts? If you introduced yourself to a potential client eating alone in a restaurant, and he asked you to join him for after-dinner coffee, would you grab the bill to make up for telling about your company? If you arranged to meet a prospect in a golf foursome, would you explain that your company is eager to send him a new set of clubs, "no questions asked"?

We hope you said "no" to all of the above. They certainly sound crass to us. And while it's difficult to set down hard-and-fast rules that cover all occasions, we can agree on some useful hints. They won't hold you back, but they'll ensure that your "power sell" does not go off scattershot.

> *You can sell to a prospect,*
> *but you can't buy him.*

Don't insult a prospect by grabbing the bill, if you have approached him in a social situation. You've both talked; you've both listened. Since the encounter was not officially set up as a sales meeting, you're under no obligation to pay. You offer to share the check, or graciously say thanks—*whichever you would do if the sales-related conversation had never occurred.*

Hint: Paying sets a price. If you insist on paying for business reasons, *you've changed the atmosphere for the worst.* You've stamped the social encounter as a business meeting. You imply that you've bought the prospect's time. You've thrown away the advantages of a social encounter—and gained nothing.

Of course, you pay when you arrange a meeting clearly designated as business-orientated. But never, **no, never,** snatch the bill and say, "Let me. It's tax-

deductible." If you're goint to pay, then pay. You don't
want to remind your guest, who may have had good
food *and* an enlightening conversation about what you
can do for him, that to an accountant he's just another
business expense.

Yes, he knows it. But you don't *say* it.

And in social encounters, he knows that you're interested in selling. The host, if it's a third party, will know
and understand—as long as it's your intent to make a
contact, not close a sale.

Hint: The operative word is "prospect."

In social situations, you can make perfectly clear *that*
you sell, *what* you sell, and *where* you sell. You can
also make clear, without much ado, that you are interested in further conversation in the appropriate setting.
Then you do something a power seller never does in
any other situation.

You back off.

That's right. In social situations, you are required to
become passive. You can comfort yourself with the
wisdom of actor John Travolta: "You can't think about
your career all the time. Life has more to offer." You
can just enjoy the party.

Well, almost.

Be on the alert for that prospect to come around looking for you. Maybe he's just shy, and doesn't know
many people—or maybe he's been to the well too many
times—or he might simply be interested. *You don't care
what his motives are; you just want to give him what he
wants—more information, a business card, or*

appointment.

And if he suggests that a business conversation might be appropriate right then and there, neglect to educate him in the rules of etiquette.

If he makes the move, fall in line!

So, whether it's Over the Wall, Down the Ladder, or Across the Table, the creative approach to potential clients takes power, but not brute force:

- You match the strategy to the prospect.
- You stay on the right side of the thin line separating courage from brashness.
- You're ready to deliver the goods the *moment* you win your opportunity.
- You *blend* business with social life, but you *do not confuse* the two.

And, most of all, you never forget that your prospect —whether at the office or seated across a banquet table—is a many-sided human being. You and your concerns might quite properly fit into one slot in their life, but only one. They're a home bird, or a church-goer, or a Dickens fan—be aware of all sides of their personality. **You should appreciate those sides, and share them, if the prospect is willing—but your aim is to play first and foremost to the side that needs you and your product.**

CHAPTER FOUR
The Real Test: Following Up
(Whiner's Excuse B: "They never had time to come back.")

The Real Test: Following Up

Rule: A prospect is a prospect is a prospect. . .and only a prospect . . . *until you make a sale.*

You haven't reached your full sales potential just because you've got all your ducks in a row: you have to make the hits. And you can't pat yourself on the back just because you've made friends through your first customers (as we suggested in Chapter One), or learned how to transform a contact from acquaintance to prospect (as we discussed in Chapter Two), or become skilled at finding prospects in unusual ways or unusual places (as outlined in Chapter Three).

If you've achieved all these things, you've made great strides. Except. . .a great stride forward, in selling, is something like being a little bit pregnant. **In the end, either you make a sale, or you don't.**

The "great strides forward" are something to tell the grandchildren about; they don't mean a thing, though, unless you have the power to make that last stride, the one that reaches the goal.

Again, you mustn't make the same mistake that many unsuccessful salespeople do: **Friends are friends, and prospects are prospects.** It's a rare human being who can be, or wants to be, both in your life. Keep the distinctions clear.

You want a friend to keep coming around because you enjoy his company. A prospect? Well, he may be one of the most charming men alive, but the joy in *his* company comes from your expectation of making a sale. Let's be clear on that. And let's not make the sad mistake of feeling good because we get invited to the country club, pleased that rich and powerful people remember our names—if we get tricked into forgetting that we are there, partly, to keep contacts alive.

It's that sense of balance.

KEEP IN TOUCH, AND STAY IN CHARACTER

As with any customer you've sold to, you want to establish regular communications with your prospects. You make the first move. And the second. And the third. . . . *But always remind your prospect, in some way that is appropriate at the time, that you are the Salesperson, not just the Mutual Friend.*

If you send Christmas cards, make sure that there's some reference to what you do. Keep a distance about as far as the title "Dr." makes when your physician signs a note or card to you. In some cases, you would want to sign yourself with your full company title. In others, you might want to make a casual reference to a conversation that took place on your sales floor, so that the image is fixed in the prospect's mind: For example, "How's that new puppy you were telling me about at the store last month?"

Remember: To the prospect, you shouldn't be the Friend Who Sells but the Salesperson Who's Friendly.

In Power Prospecting, you decide what the definitions of this relationship should be, and you always act strictly within them. The prospect will get the point. He'll appreciate the guidelines.

The Real Test: Following Up

*In short, keep in touch, but never
let your prospect think that you love
him for himself.*

You like him, sure, but you both have your own friends.
You keep in touch because you're still trying to find that
sale that will benefit both of you; that's your definition
of friendship with a prospect.

WORK THE CROWD

A hooked prospect may be most useful because of
his friends swimming around nearby. While the prospects you're close to may not be buying, what about his
contacts? *Don't hesitate to leapfrog!* Don't wait until a
prospect becomes a customer before you go after his
circle of co-workers and acquaintances.

In a small town, small talk comes easy. You run into
a friend of the prospect and you can say, "Hey, Bob was
down at the office the other day, and we had good talk
about industrial refrigeration. You and I ought to get
together some time soon." Did Bob buy? No, but you
didn't say he did. You didn't even imply it, although
you'd be pleased if this third party inferred that some
kind of deal was made.

You can use the same technique in a letter. Say a
prospect mentions his contacts in the industry, or talks
about someone he found interesting at a sales conven-
tion halfway across the country. There's your entrée,
and your very honest letter begins by mentioning that

"Bob was just sitting here in my office, discussing our latest equipment, and . . . ." You can take it from there.

Any reason to mention someone's name is a *good* reason to mention someone's name;

There's power in the most
casual connection.

More than half the time, people don't even process the information; they just recognize that you and Bob were together in a relaxed sales interview, and that's enough to give you legitimacy. The way the mind works, the third party will imagine that you and Bob grew up together in the sandbox by the time he's decided whether or not to buy from you.

In any event, the entrée is just that. You have to supply the main course, and all the rest, down to the last whiff of coffee and brandy. You don't make the contact because you want to discuss Bob; you're setting up talk about your service or product.

Use the contact, and then move on. The mention of the contact is a turn-on. You take the action from there.

CLOSE IN

We don't think negative feelings ever help, *but* you shouldn't be satisfied until the prospect becomes a customer.

Rule: Make every bridesmaid a bride. Bring 'em to

The Real Test: Following Up

the altar.

Okay, you can't make it happen 100% of the time. (Well, we think you can, if you don't back off, but we'll allow you that one in a thousand, say.) You've got a prospect who hangs around, and brings you other prospects, and buys you lunch now and then, and is good company. Why not be satisfied?

Because he hasn't bought anything!

If you need an explanation of that reason, then you should see your physician right away; something's happened to your "primordial capitalist urge," and you need help fast.

A prospect who hasn't bought should stick in your craw, set your teeth on edge, make you count the grey hairs, send you back to the sales manuals, and in all ways experienced, put misery in your days. Some things are ordained to be in their proper places.

Fish gotta swim, birds gotta fly,
and you gotta turn prospects
into customers.

No reason needed. You just gotta. It's not that you feel your self-esteem being threatened, or anything of that negative sort. It's just that your job is to sell, and you haven't sold this one guy. That's got to rankle.

It's not sane, maybe, but that's the way successful people think: Not "Look what I did today" (although it's a wise thing to take pride in your work, when it's earned) but "Look what I haven't done yet!" One more goal . . .

Of course, we aren't talking about the prospect who happens along one day to your tractor business, has a nice chat, and then announces that his farm is being foreclosed. He doesn't need you as a salesman.

But if you have something that most people want, and your prospect falls into the universal category of "most people," *the reason he isn't buying is probably you.* Or your lack of ingenuity in persuading him to buy. Or your deafness in hearing what he's really looking for.

Meanwhile, a long-term prospect becomes a liability. At first, he brings other people in, but after a while, they will begin to wonder: He brought us along, but how come he never buys anything himself?

All the more reason to sell to him, or dump him. Dumping is the easy way out, and it's a loss. So, sell.

In fact, take the direct approach.

Ask what you're doing wrong.

That's right. No games, nothing to hide. Come right out and say, "Hey, we've been talking about my products off and on for several months, am I doing something wrong? Why haven't I convinced you to buy this beautiful red Persian rug?"

It works. Maybe the prospect won't be able to answer you right away, because he may not have figured it out himself. Maybe, in fact, you just haven't been all that forceful in closing him, and he didn't realize that the time had indeed come to lay down his money.

The Real Test: Following Up

Probably he'll go away and return, saying something like, "Well, Amy and I just hadn't got around to talking about it, but we're interested, and if you're wanting to make that sale, just bring out the order book."

Sound like a fantasy? It isn't, and here's why: Despite everything we've said about remembering that a friendly prospect is a customer, first of all, most salespeople get lazy about working such a prospect. They take things for granted. They are not happy about pushing the sales angle too often. **They just forget the obvious:** *You have to ask a person to buy your product.* You don't wait for them to take the hint. You ask. Of course you know that, but sometimes people forget that basic sales principle when they're dealing with a friend of a friend, or an acquaintance made in a social setting.

The prospect won't become a
customer if you forget that he's
a prospect.

CHAPTER FIVE
Ricochet Power: Ten Ways to Help Prospects *Find You*!

1) Caught unawares, in their natural habitat:

Small town or large city, your area is likely to have good local coverage of community events. Even major national newspapers have provincial editions, because that's where reader interest takes a special turn, and the potential for you is unbounded. A club announces new officers, and perhaps you have a product that will appeal to that club—at a discount. Graduations and other special events offer obvious opportunities, but don't overlook the obvious.

When your picture's in the paper, do you ever have enough copies for all of the family? No one ever does, and most newspapers don't keep extra copies on hand for very long. *When you see a prospect pictured, just cut out the article and send it to him, with your compliments and an offer to sell.* It's a small gift that shows thoughtfulness and should give you a fine entree.

2) Likely targets, right under your feet:

A builder in the Northeast passes out his business card to the men and women who work in the local petrol station. Just because, like Everest, they are there? That's part of it, but there's another reason—and it's the height of practicality.

He discovered that these garages are in an area where many people are buying their council houses. He knows that not only do these people want to put their own stamp on their property but they have the money to pay for it as well. By doing a good job at the right price he can get his company known not only among these people but their relatives and children as well. It's word of mouth that will help spread this news, better than any advertising. . .*Find out who has a special advantage for paying for your services, and go after them.*

3) Time on their hands:

You know the old story: You spend more money when you have nothing to do. Who, near you, has very little to do? Holidaymakers? Retired folk? Firemen on call in the station house? Ski instructors in mid-July? Of course, you don't want to waste your valuable time with people who only want to be entertained. There's a fine line here.

On the other hand, people with time on their hands are likely to have dreams. . .or to be ready to have dreams inspired within them. The bored security guard might want a portable pocket-size TV set, or the firemen might want to set up elaborate electric trains while they wait for the sirens to go off. Or do you sell something that would appeal to the millions of football widows in high season, to the tired commuters who take long train rides daily? *The more bored they are, the more likely they'll be to want the escape you offer,* whether it's a week in florida, or a computer, or a good book.

4) From the top down:

When you've targeted a certain kind of customer, and you're sure that your product will be either very desirable or very useful to that type of person, consider this possibility: His boss might think so, too.

A company benefits when its customers are satisfied

and productive—and safe. You might show an executive how his support of, say, home insulation or a very efficient new air conditioner will help his employees save money at home. . . .or how a safety feature on an automobile will help save lives. . . .or how a word processor in the home could lead to increased employee productiveness.

In many cases, the employer will put some money down because he believes in the benefits of the product. In others, he may just want to help employees get what they want. *Either way, you should try to come up with an incentive plan that helps you both, one that increases your business while making it possible for the employer to become involved.* Remind him that a healthy employee is a happy employee is a productive employee. . . .

5) Knowledge is sales power:

What do *you* know, that *other* people want to know? There is probably a tremendous hunger for resource people throughout your community. If you sell computers, you know about the technology that many people still fear but find fascinating. . .if you sell clothing, perhaps you know what makes men and women look more attractive to the opposite sex. . .if you sell anything and everything, then you know about selling— about presenting yourself, communicating ideas, using powers of persuasion.

You know something that other people want to know. Find your forum, and you find more prospects. It could be a meeting of a business professionals' club, or a local talk show on late-night television, or a guest appearance at the high school. When you define yourself to others, and let that definition be linked with your business, it's a powerful way of reaching out to new prospects. *Make yourself available whenever anyone needs a speaker. The exposure will produce sales.*

6) Closer to home:

Of course, the best new prospects are the ones that come your way through contact with your satisfied customers. But you can speed the process along. Suppose that Customer A, who lives on Oak Street, is pretty happy with the sailboat he got from you, and you have a good idea that it sits out in the driveway most days, gleaming in the sun. Send little notes to his neighbours, brief and to the point: "Customer A tells me he's happy with the new boat I sold him; why not come in and talk with me about one that suits your own tastes?" Naturally, you don't want to get into invidious comparisons about price and so on, at this stage of the game, but you want to make one point very clear: *You're willing to help someone keep up with the Joneses.*

And if the neighbours don't get along? That can work to your advantage, too; you can direct your new prospect to a purchase that will *surpass* the Joneses. The product doesn't have to be out in the open for this technique to work. You can just suggest, without invading anyone's privacy, that a neighbour consult Customer B about your help in finding the appropriate heating pump or kitchen curtains. In this case, of course, you should ask Customer B's permission. He may have a reason to pretend that he has not been making purchases recently.

7) Piggy-back the costs:

Local groups will come to you for ads in theater play-bills or souvenir football game programs, and these can work very well for most businesses. But you can do better. Look at your own mail, or find out about the mail that comes unsolicited to your pool of customers. What stands out? What seems to be worthwhile? What really deserves attention?

Perhaps, in your community, there is an annual club car wash for charity or a Christmas tree sale that is generally respected. *You can offer to help with the rising costs of mailing out announcements about the event, in exchange for a note inside or a mention on the envelope* —something tasteful, but a phrase that associates you with helping. You don't want to be involved with mail no one opens, however, or with the kind of mailing that people resent. Choose carefully, and choose honestly, and the investment will pay you in new prospects.

8) The bird in hand:

In prospecting, it's a mistake to forget that a customer who's been satisfied is still a prospect. He bought one of your products, but he might find use for another. There are several strategies. He might need more than one, or he might like his so much that he can be inspired to buy one as a gift for someone else. Or he might need a second one for the summer house. . .or a slightly different one for the basement. . .or a less expensive one for his son at college. You get the idea. *All too often, the noncreative salesman just assumes, without thinking about it, that one customer per product is a good rule. Never make that assumption,* even when the product is a custom-designed sit-down lawnmower with a portable telephone and bar. Couldn't he keep another one on hand, in case the first needs to be serviced?

9) Keep your tail wagging:

The old term "bird-dogging" might not sound complimentary, at first hearing, but it's a fine tradition in sales. You sell someone a new compact disc player; obviously, your friend who owns a shop that sells laser discs will appreciate having the customer steered in his direction.

But don't just wait for the obvious barks and yelps. *Bird-dog creatively.* Think hard about the connections that don't immediately come to mind, and check them out. *You can even bird-dog with the competition,* if you have similar products that appeal to different types of customers. After all, you want to have a firmly established identity for who you are and what you do. If you send five customers who want cheap guitars to the competition, you are not losing five customers if you handle only the finest equipment. On the contrary—you're gaining a friend at the other shop who will someday send *you* a customer, and you've spread the word that you handle only the best. You've made clear who you are, and people will be back when they're ready for what you have to offer.

The customer you send away may grow into a pros-

pect in the future, when his situation improves. There are many ways to bird-dog, and you can learn some just by listening to your customers. What do they do with your product? Where do they use it? What other business benefits when you make a sale, and vice versa? The answers will give you the scent.

10) The social-science approach:

It has been said that social class is to modern-day society what sex was to the Victorians: no one talks about it, but most people are pretty sure that it's really there. *You should know the social demographics of your most likely customers, and work from that basis.* How much do they have to make to afford your service, and how much education are they likely to have, and where are they likely to live? Once you know the answers to those questions, you know the avenues to use to find new prospects.

If your target is the country-club set, you don't put your money into 10-second spots on a rock station. Instead, you follow the leader. Associate yourself with something that is very important to your target audience, whether it's the horse show or the hockey game, the regatta or the Renaissance Fayre. If you are after birds of a particular feather, find where they flock together. And don't be lazy. If you work a high street store, your customers will self-select themselves, but where are they coming from? They're only the tip of the iceberg. You've got to reach out into those suburbs, the ones that produce the bulk of your customers.

Selling takes many different skills, but, says Don Phelps, an area sales manager, "Half the battle is choosing the right prospect. If the target's wrong, the objective's wrong, and your best shots are going to go wild." *Step back and analyse the characteristics of the customer you need, then find out where he lives, where he finds entertainment, what he respects.* You get to the individual by going to the class. Prospecting requires that you learn which fields are most likely to set the geiger counter ticking.

AFTERWORD

Afterword

Power prospecting requires courage, as you must realize by now.

Our suggestions have not been easy to carry out. They take work, and they take original, creative thought. They are given in the belief that ambitious salespeople are willing to walk the extra mile, just as they always have been in this country.

These are exciting times in sales, for the salesperson who is flexible and views change as a challenge rather than a threat.

You may find yourself moving from one company to another several times in your career, as the economy changes. You may find yourself given the opportunity —and that's the proper word—to represent an industry that is just beginning today, to sell a product that is right now little more than a few scribbles on someone's design board.

You are in a career, therefore, that requires people of determination and self-confidence. It requires you to power yourself over unexpected obstacles and power your prospects into relationships that work for you.

We want you to be a powerful presence in selling, but not a hard, unfeeling person. We want you to be proud, but not arrogant—because every successful person realizes how tough the struggle can be. We want you to be prepared; there is knowledge to be learned: **Power selling is educated selling.** You don't work on pure instinct; you learn a craft.

We can give you a new approach. We can set down some hints based upon sales experience. But in the final analysis, what you become is up to you. You'll be your own power source, your own generator. And you'll also be the governor of that power, the one who makes the decisions about how to use your energies and when to conserve your growing strengths.

The future looks dazzling to us, and we think that sales people have important roles to fulfill.

Luck to you!

PART THREE: POWER PHONING

INTRODUCTION TO PART THREE

Introduction

Just how good are you? Say you're an ace at the face-to-face encounter. And you know how to get across a whole novel in right-on body language. You've learned how to get maximum power from the gifts you have for successful salesmanship.

Fine. But this is the last quarter of the twentieth century, and personal contact is becoming more extinct with every passing day. A few salespeople still work door-to-door, and thousands work in salesrooms, of course, and personal contact is the secret of much selling on the road—*but,* between you and the customer, there is likely to be a machine, at least half the time.

We're not talking just about telephone sales, which is a specialized skill. **We're talking about all sales, and it's the telephone through which you seek out prospects on a hot tip.** When you want to set up meetings or trigger the memories of a customer you pleased in the past, you usually go to the phone.

With the telephone, you hopscotch across the country, chasing down leads. You have to get information for a customer, and that's not always a piece of cake. You have to deal with repairmen or directors, bankers or deliverymen—and all of these telephone contacts require the same kind of vigour you bring to personal encounters.

But look at the disadvantages, from the salesperson's point of view:

- **The other guy doesn't have a face,** so you can't use your skills in reading his thoughts and psyching out his unconscious motives. . .

- **You don't have a face, either,** so some of the charm and persuasive power you've developed is suddenly diminished. Whether your style is based upon the wide grin or the friendly wink, a sympathetic smile or a sober look of concentration, it's lost over the telephone wires—at least, for the near future. . .

- **You can't reach out and touch.** You can't use body language, or clap someone on the shoulder (*if* that's your natural style); you can't gesture to a fine point, or touch a soft blanket. You are, quite literally, only a disembodied voice, and you're in danger of becoming sound without substance. . . .

- **You don't control the setting.** In Power Selling, you always want to be in control of the situation. You are the director. You are, in a word, the manipulator. But how do you achieve that end over the telephone, when you don't know who is in the room, or what effect the room is having on the mood of the person on the other end of the line?

With all these disadvantages, from the traditional point of view, how can a Power Salesperson make effective use of the telephone?

And remember: The telephone's only the beginning. With other devices, you may find yourself no longer talking with someone but "interfacing." *Today, messages are more and more frequently transmitted between two or more people sitting at computer termi-*

Introduction

nals. You don't even have the use of that instrument you've developed for your own ends over the years: your unique and flexible voice. How do you take charge of the action when all you have at your command are the words upon a screen?

Rule: *Don't let technology become a barrier.*

Electronic devices are springing up everywhere, just as the telephone did, because of one thing: *efficiency.* Electronic communication is efficient because of its speed (the speed of light, and you will never beat that), and its accuracy, which should be 100%, if all parties are alert and listening to one another.

Be grateful for the speed and accuracy. Take them for granted. . .*but compensate.*

The loss, in telephonic communication, is in personal appeal—expression, gesture, movement, intimate contact, physical sharing. You must compensate for that.

The gain, aside from the efficiency, is concentration on the voice, on what is being said and how it sounds.

In other words, one of your most important tools, usually just a part of your kit, has to become your most important tool. What you have expressed before in other ways has to be powerfully compressed into the voice alone. It has to have gestures, and it has to make your expressions. It has to tease out responses.

And it has to set the context of the relationship between you and the customer or prospect, whether or not the two of you will ever see each other face to face.

Power Phoning is a completely separate technique of selling, even though the aims are, as always in sales:

- To project yourself powerfully into the potential of the situation;
- To be ready to take advantage of each gain you make; and
- To take your customer or prospect in the direction that will work to mutual benefit.

Let's look at the secrets of that critical aspect of Power Selling: Power Phoning.

CHAPTER ONE
You Are Your Voice

You Are Your Voice

For Power Phoning, your voice has to radiate self-confidence, but it cannot have an abrasive or piercing timbre. It has to be capable of warmth, but avoid smarm. It has to be light, when that's what's needed, and clearly to the point when you are conveying factual information.

It has to be a portrait of you in sound.

Remember when you took assessment of yourself to begin Power Selling? You played to your strengths, worked to eliminate weaknesses. You decided for yourself what kinds of sales techniques were true to your talents and your personality. You didn't make the mistake of copying gestures, or expressions, or attitudes that were not powered naturally from within you.

The same approach is necessary for developing your phone personality. Think about it.

- You *are* how you *sound.*
- They *meet* what they *hear.*
- The *salesroom* is the *customer's head.*

To take over the atmosphere of that salesroom, you have to work hard to ensure that, over the telephone line, your voice resounds with the same uniqueness of personality that you carry when you walk into a sales situation.

Should it be deep? Should it be flippant? Should it sound like a film star?

It should be you.

Work with a tape recorder; they're dirt cheap these days, and they're so portable that you can turn to them wherever you are, whenever there's a spare moment.

Take the advice of professional actors. The first time you hear your voice on tape, resist cardiac arrest. Unless you're one of the world's happiest egoists, you won't be completely pleased with the sound. "Is that me?" is the reaction of most people. And a great many people, as you know, cannot bear to hear themselves on tape, even when they love seeing themselves on videotape or film. Why? Because with films, one is able to come across with all the resources of personality, just as the salesperson does in the one-on-one sales encounter. With sound tape, one is restricted to that one resource, just like the salesperson on the telephone.

But you don't have the luxury of turning off the machine just because your voice doesn't please you. You have a challenge—the challenge of working on it, of making improvements, and developing control.

BREAK DOWN THE VOICE ON PAPER

List the good points, and the bad. And be honest with yourself—not too self-conscious, not too willing to ignore possible faults. Aim for the positive as well as the negative. If you sound too rushed, or don't pronounce certain consonants clearly, make a note. . .but also be sure to note that you have a sincere and pleasing lilt in your delivery, or that your natural pitch has a compelling warmth.

Learn to listen for how you look. Decide how to change the image to fit the real you, by emphasizing what is most personal in your voice and delivery.

Ask for advice from a stranger or from an enemy, or from a voice professional (anybody but a friend). The first thing you have to learn is that your voice probably sounds worse to you than to anyone else, because you have false expectations. You may have thought, for example, it was a dark baritone of some character, but a tape shows that you muddy the effect by pronouncing indistinctly. Yet an unbiased observer—that is, listener —can help you with a balanced assessment. They don't have your expectations; they should be more able to hear what is really there.

When you identify the strengths and weaknesses of your voice, take the sensible approach to improvement:

> *Don't worry about what cannot or*
> *should not be changed overnight,*
> *and get right to work on what can*
> *be improved with practice.*

A strong regional accent will take quite a bit of time and effort to eradicate, but noisy breathing habits, or a tendency to drop pitch at the end of every sentence, or a problem with clearly pronounced s's are easier to concentrate on right away.

You're not an ctor, you say?

Nonsense! You must hone your tools to their sharpest. And the First-Impression Rule works on the telephone just as it does in the flesh. **The first impression is the strongest impression.** Sure, you can overcome it, but why make problems for yourself? It takes you quite a while to build up serious respect on the sales floor if you make your entrance by slipping on a banana peel. If you begin a telephone conversation with a nasal whine, you will probably never get past the unpleasant entrance.

Yes, that's what your first word is—an entrance. What the other person hears is what he sees. To them, as we've said, that voice is *you*.

DOUBLE YOUR ETIQUETTE QUOTIENT

You not only have to realize what people expect from a polite telephone conversation—and there *are* some strict rules—but you also have to realize, if you have a national market, that:

> *Telephone etiquette is different*
> *in various regions of the country.*

What sounds businesslike in the city, for example, may be thought rude in the back woods. On the other hand, the slow build of a phone conversation in a small town may be taken as time-wasting or even sarcastic by a hard-pressed business professional in a hard-driving urban centre.

These things you will have to learn from the locals. What's considered polite in one town may be considered less so across the river. Depend upon your ear, and keep listening for nuances.

But some rules are universal:

Identify yourself right away! Unless you're making an obscene phone call, there's no reason to keep your identity in reserve. Do you wear a mask when you enter the salesroom or visit a client in his office? There's nothing to be gained in anonymity. Trying to catch the customer off guard? There's no good reason to, and you just anger him by seeming to be shifty.

Let your voice paint the portrait, let your words give the details. You are somebody with a powerful message. Say so. Take the initiative. Don't hang back. Whether it's "Hi there!" or "Hello" or "How you doing?" that's considered the proper introduction in your sales area, follow the greeting with, "This is Power Salesperson X." You may only want to say the words "Power Salesperson" to yourself, but say the rest loud, and say it clear.

And state your business: If a client's worth your time, he has not got much time. You have to take that attitude, anyway. Right off, in the way you come to the point, you're letting your man know that you think he's too important for time wasting. When you explain who you are and what you represent, you are signalling that you're in the mood for business. You will be wanting answers. You will be prepared to ask questions.

Name and purpose, politely and clearly stated—in those few seconds you have made a first impression. You have established the tone of the conversation; you are well on your way to setting the ground rules.

Whether talking to a receptionist or Chairman, you have to be in character — the image of the Power Salesperson. You've got to be so secure in your role that other people believe. Your voice has to project confidence, but more than that: you are someone with a job to do. You're not abrupt, but you are brief and to the point. You're friendly, but you don't waste time on long-winded pleasantries.

And all the time, you should have your antennae out. Even in the first minute or two of the conversation, you should be listening. You've got your script in your head, but you know that you have to tailor it for the individual encounter. When you're face to face with someone, it's easier. Over the telephone, though, you might have to take a few shots in the dark before the signals begin to clear up.

Which brings us to the next chapter on the importance of listening.

CHAPTER TWO
What You Hear Is What You Get

Learning to listen may sound like a passive act.

That's actually backwards thinking. Learning to listen is a *powerful* action; it is power held in reserve, and tamed to your ends, but it is real power nonetheless.

And the results! Over and over, you will hear successful salespeople say that their real secret is that they know how to listen. If you listen well, the customer might think you agree with him, or he might think that you are simply enthralled with the force of his thinking or the beauty of his language. He just feels good.

And don't we all? Anyone who listens to our point of view must be pretty sharp, right?

The trouble with telephone sales is that you don't have facial cues to help you. Is there a pause because the customer is thinking of the right word? If you think not, then you'll probably interrupt him. But if you wait for him to speak, and he's waiting for you, he'll be made uneasy. And an embarrassed person is an angry person.

Language will give you clues, and a sense of regionalisms. In some parts of the country, a speaker will clearly come to a halt after making his point. In others, there may be one thought, a pause, and then a reworking of the thought, then a pause. . .and so on. It takes experience to hear these differences.

Rule: *He's listening to you, too!*

You can doff the passive role, when appropriate, and give your own sound cues. You can help the conversation go forward by avoiding misunderstandings. Make it clear that you have finished a sentence. End it firmly. Or end with a question for your customer. Don't let him risk embarrassment by interrupting you because you haven't finished a thought or have left a sentence hanging in midair.

SILENCE IS NOT EMPTINESS

Work on identifying the various kinds of silence—that's where your powers will *really* come into full play.

Can you tell the difference between stunned silence and an angry burn? Between a moment when the customer doesn't know what to say, because he's thinking or confused, and a moment when the customer has had his attention diverted elsewhere and is simply not listening to you?

Out of context, there would be no way to tell the difference between these various silences, all of them blank in sound. But in *context,* you can learn to make very educated guesses. The character of a silence is determined by what has gone before and by what follows. You have to rely on intuition, and on experience.

It's more natural than you might think. And if you've been involved in the personal give-and-take of the sales experience, you already have most of the necessary skills.

The danger is that you may forget to use what you know.

Listen well to the *words*. Listen twice as attentively to the silences. That's where the action may be.

What You Hear Is What You Get

When it comes to the words, listen to *how* a thing is said, as well as to *what* is said. There are many kinds of "no," and many kinds of "yes." When you are face-to-face with someone, you can tell by gestures and other clues how to interpret his words. On the telephone, you have to listen to the expression in the voice.

Special clues:

- Are there subjects that the customer is clearly avoiding?
- Is there an ironic tone to his use of your product's name?
- Does he speak forthrightly, or does he hesitate?
- If you ask a direct question, is there a pause before the answer?
- Does he sound distracted, as if he's taking opinions from someone else?
- In the picture his voice makes in your mind, what is fuzzy? Missing? Contradictory?

You know what you need to know—you just have to turn sound into picture.

And don't forget what you learned at your mother's knee. "Please" and "Thank you" and "May I?" are much heavier on the phone. When you say them, you are heard. Every word is heavier, but courtesy words are especially so. And your interlocutor hears the tone behind them: sincerity, or lack of feeling—whichever's there.

Listen for the effect that your courtesy has upon the customer.

Show that you are being polite, not putting yourself down like a doormat, and he will respond with respect. Show that you understand that courtesy is the social form of the Golden Rule, and he will understand that you expect to be treated as you are treating him.

*Courtesy, over the telephone,
is a badge of honour.*

In the right tone of voice, it announces that you know the rules and you expect them to be followed.

To put it bluntly, *courtesy is your way of saying that you do not intend to be given short shrift.*

If you can behave with circumspection, so can your customer. You mean to conduct the conversation on a gentlemanly "level", to use the old phrase, whether you are man or woman.

Listen closely, and you will hear him sizing you up: You've got the advantage on that score. He doesn't know what you look like, what you wear, or even your exact age. You've got him off-centre on those points. Listen, as he tries to sound you out.

It works both ways. And if you're conscious of that, of the way the power game works on the telephone, you can take control of the whole conversation. You see, when you're listening closely, you're gathering information that's important for your purposes. But when *he* begins to listen, and you hear him listening, you can work your will.

What You Hear Is What You Get

*The power in Power Phoning comes
from knowing how information
comes through the voice.*

The power comes from being able to listen with profit
. . .and then understand how the listening to the listening can be even more profitable: When is he paying the
most attention? What does he ask? What parts of conversation cause him to pause before replying? When
does he reply without taking time to think—and when
does he take a long time to consider exactly how to express himself?

In his behaviour are a thousand clues, but the best
come from your understanding of when the customer is
listening to you, and why.

YOU'RE NOT ON CANDID CAMERA

So, take notes. Document what you're learning as you
listen: Note down exactly what the customer is saying
to you.

Just a minute. Wasn't sales telephoning supposed to
have all these disadvantages? Maybe. But it allows you
to concentrate on a few skills, while taking advantage of
some unique opportunities. You don't wave a pencil in
a customer's face. It would make him nervous, and
probably give him the idea that you can't remember
things very well.

The truth is, you can't—unless you're one in a mil-
lion. No one remembers very well, as any good defence

lawyer knows. Witnesses remember what never happened. And any reporter knows that some public figures are certain that they've been misquoted, even after a tape of the exact wording has been played back to them.

We don't hear ourselves, and we can't take in everything someone else is saying, *and* remember it all—particularly when we have other things to be concerned about, like appearance and what we're going to say next.

DOODLE TO A CLOSE

But Power Phoning frees you to work with a pad. Did he say £5,000 ten minutes ago? You have the notes right in front of you. Did he say he's just come from having lunch at the Horse and Hounds on Cavanaugh Avenue? Bring it up later, or in a letter. Meanwhile, your're working out the numbers that will help you deliver the goods to fit his needs, and you're ready when it's time to talk.

Simple technological tools, pencil and paper. But they can make for a very impressive telephone image. You're the salesperson who remembers what he's told and who can shift the numbers around to make them work for both of you.

But this is all achieved in the protective silence of the telephone situation.

You take the credit for prodigious memory. *You don't give the secret away!*

Which is more impressive? (A) "Yes, sir, you said

457 eyebolts; I know, because I noted it down when you said it" or (B) "The eyebolts you need, I believe you said 457 or so, can be. . ."

Can it be said too often? **We all love someone who listens to us.** And if a salesperson not only listens but also *remembers?* Well, the customer owes you something already.

So play this telephone advantage to the hilt.

> *Don't let anything important escape your pencil, and bring it up later in the conversation in a* relevant *way.*

Also, have all appropriate materials nearby, or a colleague or helper who can go search out information. If the customer says, "Well, we really wouldn't be able to make a decision until you searched up Facts I, II, and III," a Power Seller, with luck on his side, could have the manual nearby which contains Fact III, and throw a note to an assistant asking for Facts I and II, which can be obtained by another phone or from an expert down the hall. Before the conversation goes very far, you can say, "Well, sir, we have all the facts you said were necessary to make a decision, and here they are." **This is the kind of thing you can't do in person,** because, on the phone, the customer isn't aware of the process; he isn't getting his defence in order.

In short, you can bowl him over.

Off guard, the customer will be primed for your next move, so close in. Over the telephone, you can marshal your resources without warning. This is a fine tactical advantage. Listen with the ears of a bat, but make sure that he doesn't understand your silences—that's the approach.

And remember: **What can't be seen isn't happening.** So don't give your secrets away. Don't let him know how you do it. Don't let him guess how you keep one jump ahead, with your trusty pencil and pad and your stacks and stacks of useful materials.

Work the shadows . . .

CHAPTER THREE
Out of Sight, Out of Range

Out of Sight, Out of Range

Far away, but right next to you: that's the contradiction of the telephone and other communications devices. Someone is on the other side of the country, but the voice is perched in your ear.

We all live with this contradiction and think nothing of it. But we make assumptions about it that could weaken the thrust of your sales presentation. Unconsciously, part of you is probably saying, "Well, he's all the way down in Cornwall. . .not really my concern." No, you don't think that consciously, but the customer *is* far away. You've got to listen to the positive side of your nature, the part that says, "But, dammit, he's right here, and I've got him [his voice, anyway] clutched in my right hand."

***He's in your hand, not a bit
farther away than that.***

Focus on him. You can move that voice back and forth. You could throw him against the wall, if that was your nature. He's in your power, as a sales prospect, and you have literally "got him on the line."

Okay, but he's not buying.

Are you going to let him get away with that?

Of course not! You're sure of what you want to sell, and you're sure of how it will fit into his business plans, and you know that you have the power to make this sell work.

What's holding it up?

GETTING THROUGH WITH
THE SMOKING GUN

You have to find the right key.

The deal's a good one, but the customer isn't taking the order. You know there's nothing wrong with the product—that's the attitude that powers a sale. You know, because you've done your research properly, that the customer *can* buy. You may have learned from listening closely that he's not happy with a current product or service.

What's wrong? Perhaps you haven't realized the necessity of giving him the "smoking gun."

You've explained why he should want the product, but perhaps you've forgotten that he works for someone else. He reports to a boss, who reports to a division head, who reports to a board.

The smoking gun is the evidence that your customer doesn't directly need, but that he needs for one of two very important reasons: to convince his superiors that his judgement is sound, before the fact, so that the sale will be approved...or to convince his superiors that his judgement *was* sound, after the fact, so he won't be made a scapegoat for problems elsewhere in the company.

Corporate politics, that's what we're talking. As a Power Seller, working most of the time on your own, you may forget just how rare and special your working independence has become. **Even heads of major corporations sometimes feel that their hands are tied**

these days, with the necessity to be responsible to stockholders and board members. Think how your customer, if he's in a large company, is caught between many opposing factors.

He needs that evidence. But he may not ask for it. He may be too embarrassed to say, "Hey, you've sold it to me, but I need such-and-such to convince the higher-ups." You have to hear him say that between the lines, from hundreds of miles away, and produce the smoking gun. Is it what he needs? You'll know in a moment. You must then give it to him; the sound you hear will be relief. . .with an appropriate tinge of gratitude.

THE ABSOLUTE WORST

The customer agrees that the product sounds perfect. He can't think of anything wrong with it. So why isn't he buying?

Intuition will have to be your guide, but maybe those strange silences over the telephone lines indicate that he needs to be told "The Absolute Worst." That's how the mind works, sometimes.

Something just sounds too good to be true. What you should have done (and will, the next time) is follow the old rule of bringing out the bad news first. The high cost, or the frequent repairs, or the likelihood of imminent obsolescence.

Of course, now, you're in a ticklish situation. You bring up The Absolute Worst, and the customer may ask, "Why didn't you bring this up before?" (And that question implies, "And how many other bad things do you have to tell me?")

But go ahead. Do it.

Your tactic? You seem to realize, all of a sudden, that something is holding your man back. You wonder if it could be the Absolute Worst, and if it is, you want him to know that there's another way of looking at it. That's the way *you* look at it, and so you don't even think about it as a disadvantage anymore. After all, people who come to your product have typically preferred its technical superiority, even with the occasional breakdowns, or have felt that the high cost could be handled in ways that bring tax relief.

Pimples? **You don't cover them up, but you try to turn them to advantage.** After all, they're an indication of hormonal change, and a harbinger of the maturity that is to follow. Put the spotlight on them; admit they're there; show that there's something good to be said about them.

Maybe—we'd say, *probably*—the customer already knew about the disadvantage. He just wanted to see if you'd bring it up and how you'd handle it.

Deal with the Absolute Worst, and you'll be dealing with a new customer.

> *He's going to respect you, if you
> admit the defect and show how it
> can be put into reasonable
> perspective.*

Out of Sight, Out of Range

RING HIS DOORBELL

You suddenly realize that, unlike you, the customer thinks there's a continent between you. He doesn't realize you have him in the palm of your hand. He doesn't realize, in a nutshell, that you and your product are really as accessible as you claim.

You have to "Ring His Doorbell"—let him know you're as close as the front door.

You're not there on the doorstep, but what about your product? Has the company down the street been a good customer, or has someone in town good reason to praise your work? Is your company known for its work in the area?

> *Somehow, you have to plant the*
> *idea that your product is a reality,*
> *accessible to him. . .even if you're*
> *sitting hundreds of miles away*
> *even in a different country*

There are too many unspoken assumptions—that the product is suited for your area, not for his. . .or that you are too far away to be responsible if something goes wrong. You have to relieve these assumptions, assumptions that won't be stated, but hidden beneath his words.

Perhaps he's the first in his area to try your service. Well, you can't avoid the truth. Since you can't emphasize accessibility, you might want to stress how unique he will be. Explain how important it is for the company to make this first inroad, and he'll get the point: You'll be going out of your way to make sure that, as the first buyer, he's happy with the product.

Or maybe you just have to know more about his town than he does. *Show him how the service is particularly good for him* because it works so well with the climate, or the transportation factors, or the tastes of the populace. (Of course, you never *tell* a man about his own area; you *remind* him, and show him what he already knows will fit into your sales picture.) If you've really got the time to do apt research, you can talk about how your product will help him avoid the problems of other companies in the area.

And remember: **You have that telephone advantage of being invisible, part of the electronic darkness.** You can have maps and reference books and atlases and newspaper articles right on your desk, for immediate reference.

Ring His Doorbell by knowing where he lives—as factually as possible.

Ring His Doorbell by showing him, in a sense, how to walk your product from the street and out of its packing crate and into full assembly-line order.

Ring His Doorbell, at the bottom line, by giving him the sense that you are in the room with him. You see the size and shape of his needs. You feel the full flavour of the town and its people. You understand the situation from his point of view and could take a walk in his boots.

SCRATCH THE DIAMOND

Everyone tries to scratch the diamond to see if it's real. Obviously this is a difficult feat over the phone. You've got to come up with the second-best thing: the accumulation of physical evidence.

If it's in the paper, it must be true: Do you have news clips about your product? Good reports in trade magazines? Don't be shy about including small-town stories that cover the opening of your local offices. If it's in the paper, it has legitimacy. There's truth in the old saw: I don't care what they write about me, as long as they spell my name right.

If they can pay, they must be good: In reasonable amounts, mail your customer copies of ad campaigns, or send along the product descriptions that you use with other sales personnel. Emphasize the ads that have good clear photos and a straightforward product message. You don't want any interference with your own message. . .which is being tailor-made for this particular customer. Ads show that your company has made an investment in the product, that they're committed to it.

If the plug's good, the cheese must be ripe: You can't always send a sample of your product, but try an approach that your customer will never forget. What works depends upon you and your aims. Sometimes, to be sure, it *might* work to hire someone to appear on your customer's doorstep in a gorilla suit and present him with some object that brings your product to mind.

Usually, however, your creative approach will be more sober and more original. Perhaps a well-made toy will bring your product to mind, or a mounted machine part will suggest the engineering marvels of your product. Anything physical that is somehow a reminder of what you have to offer is a good supplement to your telephone campaign. It brings you into the room. It is an objective proof that you exist, but you have to power your way into many other levels of customer consciousness. *Objects jog the memory. They exist, you exist.*

OTHER BARRIERS

Each situation may introduce you to another hidden reason for customer resistance over the telephone. Always, you are translating your sales knowledge to the special challenges and restrictions of telephone contact.

You find the problem by means of the customer's voice, but you deal with it in terms of his physical situation.

Consider the customer to be in the palm of your hand, ready to be directed, but remember that he sees himself as being far away and easily cut off.

So put some physicality into your own conversation—weather, clothes you're wearing, the colour of the rug on the floor — to give yourself reality . . . but relate consistently to *his* physical reality, even if you don't have many hints about it. (*Never* forget that it's sunny in Aberdeen, if he mentions it, for example;

that's an event for him, and you should recall it at the end of the conversation.)

Check the weather in the morning paper, for a start. It's a simple thing, but think how surprised you'd be if someone called from miles away and remarked on the temperature where *you* are (or the local football game). **You've got to project yourself physically into the customer's backyard.**

And never forget to ask that basic sales question: *Why aren't you buying?* If you haven't figured out what the problem is, go to the source. The customer knows why he isn't buying. Usually, he'll tell. Often, you can do something about it. You just need that clue to follow, when nothing is coming across the telephone line.

Or should you call it intermission, and try again later?

That's the subject of the next chapter.

CHAPTER FOUR
When to Call

ON THE HUNT FOR PROSPECTS CLOSE TO HOME

Even if you don't intend to make your pitch over the telephone, you have to develop your own script for scouting prospects in your town.

Obviously, you should look for other means of contact, when possible, because then you can bring all your talents to bear upon the prospect. But if he's busy, or you live in a large town, it may be that the telephone is the most direct approach.

You have to initiate. You have to state your business and lay it out on the line.

> *Your goal is not to make a sale,*
> *but to arrange a meeting.*

You have a "soft" assignment, in a sense. You're not asking that much of a commitment—just the consent to come in for a look-see.

On the other hand, make sure the casual arrangement has underpinnings of steel. This is just a visit to the shop, or the sales floor, but make sure that you have time and date down pat. Have it so certain—and repeat the particulars—that you won't be out of line to call later, in case your prospect doesn't show, and ask with concern what happened.

Concern, that is, not anger.

Your role in prospect calling is to make yourself available for discussion. You are trying to make opportunities happen.

CEMENTING A RELATIONSHIP

The best customers are the ones who have already bought from you. They will buy again.

The telephone is an intimate, casual and inexpensive way for you to build a long-term relationship with customers. You don't want to harass them, of course, but there are legitimate occasions for calling. A six-month checkup, or a special sale, or a sudden drop in interest rates—the reason will depend upon the product.

And you are, thanks to common sense, drawing a fine line between keeping the customer informed and suggesting that he become satisfied with what he recently bought. Your tactics for the life of the product are to check up on the performance and to offer help with service problems. Within a logical period of time, you may begin suggesting—not that he *replace*—but that he *upgrade*. It's not that the first product is falling apart; it's that he is in a position to appreciate a better item.

In certain circumstances, it is even appropriate to call with condolences when there is a death in the family, or with congratulations, if the event is really special and publicly known.

Remember: *You are usually calling a family, not just one person.* You're tying up the line, if only for a few minutes, so you better make sure you don't waste anyone's time. You ought to find out when most people in your customer's social class and neighbourhood are likely to eat, or watch television, or go to evening church services. Always remind yourself of the obvious. You are trying to make yourself memorable, not an annoyance. Keep those ears wide open for the unspoken news that you are calling at a bad time. Hit and run, that's the idea. Say your piece, cover the embarrassing silences and leave while they're waiting for more.

WHEN THERE'S NO OTHER WAY

In some sales situations, the telephone is the only possible instrument of communication.

How do you start? This depends upon the importance of your prospect. As we've already suggested, Power Phoning is fuelled by research beforehand, when it's going to pay off. You're a voice from the void, but you should know as much as you can about who you're calling and what he probably needs. You should know something about his town and the way life is lived there. Most importantly, you should have a very good idea, before ever lifting up the receiver, about just how well your services are going to mesh with the needs of the prospect.

All right, you can't always know all of these things. But you can come closer than most salespeople do, if you view that phone call as the climax of a campaign— not the whole enterprise.

> *You've got to build up to the phone*
> *call, just as you would prepare*
> *yourself to enter a customer's office.*
> *Same process exactly.*

You've got to have a game plan in mind. You've got to buoy yourself up to a peak of self-confidence. You've got to *know* that you are on top of the situation. Some people even feel more professional if they are sitting up straight at the desk, tie carefully knotted, as if they can be seen. Yes, that can help. *But it shouldn't distract you from the real appearance, the appearance of your voice.*

Do you gargle? Spray your throat? Run over a few scales? Well, none of this could hurt. The real secret to a strong voice, though, the kind that impacts across the wires, is very simple—and, we're sorry to say, like most secrets to success, it takes some work. **Voice teachers agree that the principal ingredient in a winning voice is good health.** If you've lost sleep the night before, you might be able to smile yourself through an interview, and few will be the wiser. But it shows in your voice.

So, with your voice in good order, and all your sales preparations run down the checklist, the problem now is . . . getting heard.

GETTING HEARD

Have you prepared the way?

Red-carpet calls: In some situations, you should have sent materials ahead, or warned your prospect by letter or telegram that you would be making a telephone call.

Another route is to call their receptionist or secretary, but don't ask to talk to him. You're making telephone *appointments,* and think that the two of you will need at least ten minutes (or whatever) for a worthwhile discussion. If the secretary won't be specific, try to find out a good time to call, and ask them to pass along the information that you will be calling that particular day. (Naturally, you don't carry this approach past logic; if the person you want to talk to is available when you're on the line, you *will* talk with them.)

This type of preparation makes the points you always want to make:

- That you're organized
- That you don't have time to waste and don't intend to waste anyone else's time
- That you are in control of your schedule—and are probably in control of a lot more than that.

Have you prepared yourself? As we've suggested, research is crucial, to the extent that it can be carried out. Information about the customer and his company, about his hobbies and his professional ambitions—well, these would be terrific.

Often you have to punt; we realize that. But you can prepare yourself to talk with the "customer-as-type"— not to belittle his individuality, but to play to those ideas and qualities that are representative of someone in his position.

You may not be able to find out anything about the customer as an individual human being, but you can probably get your hands on a trade publication that they would read. You may not be able to find out much about the actual operation of your prospect's plant, but you can find out about similar operations.

And, with an ear alert to the need for a quick rewrite, you have your script in hand. . .and have tested it for telephone viability. You know what points you want to make, and you have broached them to yourself on the tape recorder we mentioned earlier. You've learned which of your pet phrases really come across with power and class, and which get lost somehow in transmission. You've decided how you want to sound, on this occasion. *You are, in the best of all possible worlds, ready to make this telephone call in your sleep.*

Have you *unprepared* yourself? Don't overdo it. If your customer doesn't want to talk about the day's stock market, don't rush ahead and show off your knowledge about gold futures. *Control your preparation; don't let it control you.*

Don't make assumptions that can insult your customer and ruin your image of control: Don't assume that they are married, and certainly don't put words or opinions into their mouth. If there's just been a local election, don't assume that you know your prospect's views or could even take a stroll through the land mines offered by a discussion of the issues involved.

You are using your preparation to control the course of a conversation the way a racing-car driver controls his highly tuned machine: on top of the steering wheel and the foot pedals with a vengeance, but listening every second for unusual sounds in the motor and chassis.

When to Call

You have to be ready to draw upon your preparation, but you don't flaunt it. *You're not on the phone to tell the person what they already know. And you're certainly not there to let them know that you think you're going to educate them.*

How's your timing?

Not only should you know when to hang up, you should know when to call again. Don't leave this critical information hanging. Ask. Make a definite appointment, to the extent that you can. If you can't name the date and the time, at least get something like "within the month" or "right after the election." Politely tell the customer that, yes, that sounds fine and you are marking it down in your appointment calendar.

To strengthen that call, give yourself and the customer an "assignment," so that each of you is working on it, already something of a team. It should be something simple, and it can be either personal or business in orientation. Say that you'll find out for certain if a certain famous sports personality really went into retirement in your town and opened a restaurant—assuming that some such question arose out of conversation. Or have your customer promise to find out the name of a certain product that failed for him, or the exact number of feet available for putting your equipment in place.

The less important, the better. This is just a way of tagging you and your upcoming call in the memory. **Rather than the person who will call again from Company X, you are the human being who had an interest in a specific thing, or could answer a trivial**

question for him. This is a kind of commitment to the next phone call.

And no Power Phoner needs to be told, at this point, that you should not only have the information he wants —which shows that you come through, even in the little things—but you should have it ringed with diamonds, because you are the type who goes the extra mile. That is, you not only found out what the sports personality is doing these days, but you got his autograph and it's in the mail.

Do you need the blindfold, or shall we just fire? Stand up and take it—that's the other time when you should reach for the telephone, without a moment's hesitation.

When you come back to the office, and there's a message about a product complaint, or your mail has an angry letter, don't wait for the carrier pigeons. *Call. Call, and do everything you can do to rectify the situation. If your company won't let you perform in this way, find another company fast.* You can't be a Power Seller if you leave a trail of dissatisfied customers behind. They have phones, too. They have friends.

We live in an age of consumerism, and everyone you deal with knows that. If you sell in a shop, your customers have a right to expect quick service, when something goes wrong. If you're dealing with business professionals, then you are dealing with men and women who have to respond to the challenges of the consumer movement, and they certainly expect to reap the benefits of it.

When to Call

*Quite apart from the ethics, and
that is fundamental, it is always
good business to call back when
there's a complaint.*

You're going to come through anyhow, so why not
come through promptly and cheerfully? Don't act as if
you're making compensation at the point of a gun. It's
your job. It's your privilege. **You're in business to
make things work, not to leave a trail of failures.**
The intimacy and immediacy of a phone call will do
much to assuage the customer's sense of loss or incon-
venience, until compensation is actually made.

AFTERWORD

Afterword

The phone sits there, a machine waiting for your touch to bring it to life.

But you can't consider it a machine. You can't look at it as an object in itself; *it is your connection with some-one else.* Through it, you project an image based upon your voice, based on your personality, fortified with your sales preparation.

Each time you approach the phone for a sales con-tact, it has to be as much an event as an appointment in the flesh. You don't pick up the receiver until you're primed. *You are at all times aware of the person on the other end and his situation.* If necessary, wear blinkers or close your eyes; you have to be where he is, bringing yourself to his understanding.

At the same time, you have all the advantages of note taking and research available to you. You should keep notes from previous conversations, if you are calling someone a second or third time. You should have your files of correspondence in front of you, if you have been exchanging letters.

You should plan the phone call
just as you plan a sales presentation
to a group or a tough new prospect.

You visualize your customer, and you try to imagine what images your conversation will bring to him. You can have written down in front of you the main points you want to make and remain determined to bring them up, when appropriate.

The trick is to concentrate on the sound that goes over the wire. . . your voice, and its pauses. The words. The implications that lie beneath the words. The image in sound.

Above all, don't let the telephone cause you to relax your businesslike manner. You can be casual and friendly, because that is surely the Modern Way of Business. . .*but you don't forget the purpose of your call:*

- Business should be taking place.
- Points should be made.
- Commitments should be made.
- Follow-ups should be scheduled.

Once you realize how to translate your Power Sales talents into the medium of the telephone, you'll understand that you already know how to sell over the telephone. **Power Phoning is just Power Selling with electronic aids.** Concentrate your efforts into beaming your talents into that tiny mouthpiece, and you will have the key to successful telephone sales.

PART FOUR: CLOSING THE SALE

INTRODUCTION TO PART FOUR

Introduction to Part Four

What *makes* your sales day?

- The customer who praises your presentation and says that he'll tell everyone he knows to come by and see you?
- The prospect who says you've certainly convinced him and that he'll get back to you as soon as he discusses your product with his boss?
- The buyer who says that he'll be needing your service in a month or two and will let you know just as soon as he's ready?

Wipe them all off the slate. They're worth nothing—except as chicken feed for a chicken ego. **What makes a power salesman's day is a sale**—and that's a signature clearly set down on the dotted line. Every salesperson agrees:

The secret to sales is the close.

You can power yourself to peak efficiency. You can power your customer up to peak interest, but, if you don't power the presentation to a sure and final close, it's a dud.

- Don't be distracted from your main goal.
- Don't forget the words to the music.

You should enjoy performing, and you should enjoy your customers as human beings. You should be pleased when you solve problems or meet objections with good arguments. You should be excited by the promise of further contacts or future sales: *but these are the sideshow.*

The main event is the *financial commitment.*

It's not enough that the customer likes the product, thanks to you—thanks to you, he must make a commitment to the product. Simply put, **he must sign.**

It's not enough that the customer really comes to believe that you are the finest sales professional in the business. **You're in the business of obtaining his signature and the money that follows.**

It's not enough that the customer has decided to buy but will return to close the deal—there's no deal *until* he signs. He may be sincere, but he can change his mind—once he's out from under the influence of your power sales approach. Or an air conditioner may fall on his head. Or he'll happen upon a better deal. Or he'll suddenly have to replace the water heater:

> *The rule is—when hungry (and your sales power-pack is charged with an insatiable hunger to do well), you don't throw a fish back into the water. You land it.*

The day's a waste, the sales encounter's probably a waste, unless you are able to close. The bottom line in sales is the bottom line. As a salesperson, you are only as good as the commitments you produce. **A sale is a signature.**

Anything else is pure show biz, and you don't make

Introduction to Part Four

commissions from song-and-dance. For optimum power in the sales encounter, you aim for a close—and nothing but. All your will and determination must focus on the close.

CHAPTER ONE
Starting the Order Blank

Starting the Order Blank

From your first words, *the sales book should be visible,* like a stethoscope around a doctor's neck. It's your badge, your symbol; it keeps before the customer the essential idea that what you do is take orders.

Don't be coy.

Gesture with the sales book. Leave it flipped open to a middle page, so that the customer can feel that he is about to join a crowd of past customers. Establish the order form as a third party in your encounter.

Have it primed: a pen or pencil should be visible and at the ready. Tap with a pen to make a point. Total up discounts or other relevant figures on the cardboard back; the message is that your pad is a portable work centre—active, alert, waiting to take orders.

Nature abhors a vacuum, and so should you.

FILL IN THE BLANKS

Begin filling out the sales slip as soon as possible—if necessary, in bits and pieces. The customer doesn't want to commit himself yet, but you could write down his name and number, *just for your records.* If he were to buy, the product would be delivered in his neighbourhood on a Wednesday, say, and you write that down. *Just for your records.* You could write down the description and price of the product, as if it's necessary to take notes so you won't forget. You could figure up the total price or the monthly payment that will be necessary—information that is critical to his final decision.

Quickly, you have completed a sales slip, lacking

nothing except that essential signature.

Does this process make the customer skittish?

Not if you proceed calmly and naturally while you continue to propel the sales conversation forward in high gear. Does the patient tell the physician to stop fiddling with his stethoscope? *The sales book is your work tool;* you let the customer know that it's in operation, but you don't struggle with it. Using it this way has to become second nature with you.

> *Old truths are dependable: actions*
> *speak louder than words.*

IN BLACK-AND-WHITE

On one level, the customer is listening to your sales pitch, thinking and feeling his way—under the power of your guidance—to the point of decision. But on another level, he is watching the sales book in operation. He may be *hearing* you discuss colour schemes or service record or warranty, but he *sees* that you are constantly working toward a sale.

- You want him to know that you want the sale.
- There's no advantage to surprise, in this case.
- The groundwork should be laid quickly.

As the two of you move around the sales floor, let him glance at what you've written. Don't wave it in his face; just **give him the opportunity to face the facts in black-and-white.** As you know, he will be weighing

Starting the Order Blank

the cost considerations, say, while you are both chatting about the problems he had with his last lawnmower. A part of the customer's consciousness will be off to the side, carrying on a dialogue with the sales slip he just saw: "£278.89 isn't so bad, since it includes taxes, delivery, and credit charges." **In other words, the moment of truth—when the £249.99 sale-price item totals to £278.89—is easier to take, if he reads it first.** This way you don't spring the total price and then have to deal with his wavering, or his embarrassment. He does all that work for you—if you subtly allow him a glance at your computations.

(This ploy leads to another, when you want to work full power on this customer. After he's seen the total on your sales slip, you can slap your brow and say, "Hey, I think I can get you X% discount." Lower the price he has just dealt with, and you've given him a sudden windfall in his mind. *He owes you.*)

Remember:

> *When you're with a customer, you're*
> *working, and when you're working,*
> *you should be using your tools.*

Keep that sales book open and that pen or pencil moving.

CHAPTER TWO
Guiding the Customer's Selections

Guiding the Customer's Selections

One crucial key to top sales power, as we've discussed in other sections in this book, is your ability to *read* the customer. *What does he think he wants from you? What does he really want? How can you match his desires with what you have to sell?*

Warning: You can't move a customer from nowhere to Point A. You can move him from Point B to Point A, so you have to *map* Point B: where he's at! *Nowhere* cannot be mapped, and there's no pathway from there to here. In other words, you have to *locate* the customer—get into his head—before you will be able to move him where you want.

Reading the customer quickly and accurately will also save you valuable sales time. There are occasions when a customer has a definite need that you *can't* fulfill. In that case, make clear what you *can* do for him, another day, and send him to someone who can help. Facilitating a sale that he needs will produce a kind of commitment; he'll remember your efficient help and probably return to you sometime. Wasting his time and yours—when you sell topcoats and he is desperate for a plumber's mate—will only give him a bad temper and you a bad name. Sometimes, you have to rein in.

Once you know what the customer wants—or what he *could* want, if you power the sales conversation to the proper goal—you've got to plan your assault upon the merchandise.

Plan is a misleading word. You must be able to instantly

*choose the specific model you mean
to sell and head toward it so
confidently and directly that there is
no dawdling along the way.*

You're implying to the customer that you have listened carefully (and we hope you have), so you *know* what he wants—and that you can act decisively, because you are *equipped* with what he wants.

Warning: Don't set yourself up for arguments. Say "I believe" or "I think we have what you want—the fire-engine red tux with sharks-teeth buttons." Why? Because when he sees the real thing, he may realize his mistake. You do *not* want to get into a wrangle over whether or not the tux is exactly what he described, and so on. You *do* want to be in the position of being able to say, "Oh, perhaps this black tux with pearl buttons would please you. It does have the same sharp Italian cut as the other, and costs a bit less." Notice that you ignore the distinguishing characteristics of the red tux—the bad taste—and shift the discussion to a more profitable area. What the customer really wanted, as you now know, is not a red tux but an unusually classy tux. You show him how your model will give him real class, without calling into question his original choice.

In other words, you lead, but you don't force. You help him to choose wisely, from what you have available. You realize that he will not vanish in smoke when he walks out the door, but will be a living advertisement—positive or negative, depending upon you—for you, your product and your company.

> *Always take the position that you*
> *are trying to fulfill the customer's*
> *wishes, even when you lead him to*
> *choices that at first seem far afield*
> *from his original choices.*

Each time, you link your suggestion to something you've learned about him in your conversation. You are demonstrating that the suggestion suits him, not just anyone. The coat emphasizes his broad shoulders, or her slender waist. The microwave fits into his swinging-singles style of living. The jeep will be useful in business.

The point is to start the customer thinking about possible relationships between himself and the product. You are setting up a marriage of man and object, and the tie that binds is the activity that will be enhanced by the sale.

Once you get the customer thinking in those directions, you can let him feel that he is taking the lead.

CHAPTER THREE
When to Let Him Take the Lead

When to Let Him Take the Lead

After you've channelled the customer's attentions in the right direction for your purposes, you can let your control loosen—let him feel a bit of space and freedom of choice.

Of course, you have carefully circumscribed the possibilities in several ways:

- You've *seized* upon the desires that you know you can help fulfill and shown how those desires can be realized with a purchase from your stock.
- You've physically *connected* him to an area of the showroom, or to a section of the product catalogue, that will concentrate his attention.
- You've *articulated* for him, very clearly and directly, what his wishes are and how they are likely to be fulfilled.

In other words, **you have engineered the sales encounter for your own ends—ignoring or discounting those wishes of the customer that you cannot do anything about.** You have formulated the guidelines of the purchase, based upon what you've been able to draw from the customer's personality. And you have staked out the limits: today, the subject is, for example, acoustic guitars and nothing else.

You have focused the decision, and that is the first step toward making the decision.

Quite naturally from this process, you have advanced from asking such general and useless questions as, "Can I help you with anything," to the useful, "Isn't this the guitar you really want?" You have your closing goal—and you can let him lead himself to it.

You play him as if he were a guitar. When he begins to centre upon the best possible purchase—from your point of view—you warm to his decision. **When he veers toward a product that is not your first choice, you cool it—letting your mood drop a watt or two, asking politely what has caught his attention.**

This is one of the most useful questions you can ask in true power selling. You don't employ a sarcastic tone, or gasp in disbelief, *but you do put the burden on him.* Why choose guitar C rather than guitar B, the one you've both agreed already produces clear sound and is easily portable? If he knows the answer, you've got a hook to use to bring him back to the sale *you* want to make. If he doesn't know the answer, you can fill in the blanks. If he is determined to buy, of course, you are pleased for him. And you can't wait for the next customer, so you can sharpen your skills of letting the customer lead you where you want him to be led.

He will think he's making the final choice, if you have:

- Focused your selling power on his desires
- Matched those desires to a supposedly ideal product
- Let him find the product for himself.

When to Let Him Take the Lead

Also, letting him *seem* to take the lead is a good double-check of your initial analysis of him. If he suddenly makes an unexpected choice, you might have missed an important element in his needs and wants. You then add the new element—if it's important—to your game plan. You may have to aim the customer towards a model that you had previously ruled out.

As the customer seems to be picking his way through merchandise, he will be looking over his shoulder, as it were, to see if your judgement backs up his. This may be an unspoken query, and you may have to answer in kind. As a follower, you can stay only a little bit ahead of the customer, when he's leading!

Letting the customer lead is a great path to the closing, if you keep him away from the detours and shortcuts. You can begin your close quite frankly: "So, this is the one you've chosen?" If it's not, the line still works a few minutes later. The point is, **when the customer begins making a selection, he should be persuaded to complete the process.** He should make the selection— and pay for it. No time like the present.

When you have him leading the sale, which you have set up, he has the responsibility of making a commitment. It's his move, if you've made the proper preparatory moves. If he's choosing, he is going to have a choice. Or so you have determined. When he makes the choice, there is no reason not to buy—none, anyway, that you can think of.

Or does he, as we discuss next, need his imagination turned up a few notches, before the final commitment?

CHAPTER FOUR
Visual Aids—A Powerful Tool

Visual Aids—A Powerful Tool

We've already talked about the usefulness of a visible sales book. It's your identification. But what about other visual cues?

YOUR PERSONAL IMAGE

Obviously, if you are selling men's clothing in a fashionable suburban shopping mall, you won't greet your customers in orange-and-green plaids. At least, not until styles take a sudden turn in a new direction. If you are selling classical records, you strive for a certain look, be it poetic scruffiness or tweedy gentility.

In other words, your whole appearance is an important visual cue, giving you credibility to the customer.

This is a difficult area, when you think about it: you can't let your taste be too advanced for the customer you want to serve, or appear to be outlandish or *superior.* If you like wasp-tailored Italian silk suits, but work in an industry where people in business never go beyond Brooks Brothers cuts, you should probably indulge your clothing tastes away from the office.

Clothes send out a message, as does your jewellery. If you have moved into a different area, find out immediately what various styles *mean.* There are two extremes: dressing *incorrectly* because you are wearing the clothing of another area, or dressing *foolishly* by trying to wear nothing but clothes that bespeak your new home. If you've just moved from London to Bradford, for example, you wouldn't want to wear wild, trendy clothes, but you also wouldn't want to deck yourself out completely in flat cap and clogs either!

Look around you, see who is
wearing what, try to find out why.

Social class, and even political preferences, are indicated by clothing. You would do well to spend quite a bit of thought in choosing the image that will bring out the most powerful forces in you.

And pay special attention to jewelry. People tend to have very strong tastes in this regard, and you will do well to note them. (By the way, though it isn't visual, you should pay close attention to your scent, if you like to wear cologne. Regional and social class tastes play a part in these matters, as well. More messages...)

SALES DISPLAYS

From visual cues about yourself as the salesperson in control to visual aids related to the product is a logical step.

Are your point-of-sale displays attractive *and* clear?

- **Do they send out a message that can be understood in a couple of seconds—in one quick**

glance?
- Has the stock been presented well? Or is the room a visual jumble more worthy of an old-fashioned pawnshop?
- Do the colours complement the colours of the product?
- Is the customer's eye naturally led to focus on individual products, or is the variety so great and confusing that he won't know where to look first?
- Is there space between displays?

Obviously, you will not be in control of some of these factors, in certain sales situations, but if you have any input at all, you must work on improving the *look* of your sales area, because the *look* helps produce the *feel*. One glance at your sales area gives an impression that appeals to more than one sense. That overall impression is a powerful calling card, for better or worse. **The visual story is the setting for the sales story.**

Pictures Make a Sale

Then, when applicable, you will want to take advantage of any **audio-visual aids** that have been produced in relationship to your product. Aptly used, they can help you bring a customer to a close.

Is the product desirable because it will heighten the pleasure of leisure activities? Well, it looks pretty lifeless on the sales floor, but pictures of it in action will set the customer's imagination alight.

Is the product designed to bring warmth and comfort to the home? It probably looks naked on the sales floor, or its effect is diminished because it is placed next to so many similar products. A Persian rug, for example, is hard to assess, when the room is chock-full of rolled-up vibrant weaving. But a photograph singles out the item—the warm red rug—and demonstrates how it will brighten a room. (It also, of course, shows the other objects of a fashionable room, adding to the sense of luxury.)

Is the product used for producing something else? Today's food photographers are geniuses at their craft, and pictures will show show the promise of the new oven. Hobby magazines will suggest what can be achieved with a new camera.

And, of course, there's always the *subliminal appeal.* **The best pictures will show your product in a context that is enviable.** You will be able to select the context that is appropriate for your customer. The high-schooler looking for a compact-disc player will not be impressed with a photo of long-haired men in cardigans serenely listening to their new device, but he might be moved by the photos of teenagers dancing at the beach, as their portable disc-player radiates tunes in the moonlight.

Visual aids, then, can help you propel the customer toward the close, although there's another technique that may be required, no matter what your method of approaching the close.

CHAPTER FIVE
Massaging the Sale

He's there—or almost there—but he won't sign.

He's clutched.

Pull back inside yourself a minute, take a deep breath, and decide that you are going to quietly take confident control of the situation. After all, if you've been doing your job, the customer is probably feeling the pressure—not the high pressure that is produced by an offensive, rushed and pushy salesperson, but **the pressure that is entirely natural when one has to make a decision.**

That's the key word: *natural.*

You've got the customer excited about the possibilities that can open up if he buys your product or service, but he has a *natural* reluctance to part with his money. As do we all. He has a *natural* insecurity about the wisdom of his decision. He has a *natural* fear that, as soon as he signs to buy from you, something better will come along.

The point is, you should be prepared for all of these *natural* fears and lack of decisiveness. *Remember:* You are in a business where knowledge of a product and the ability to make a buying decision are expected skills. You've trained yourself to know the field, and you've powered your inner abilities in the direction of fast, accurate, and effective decision making. **Most people don't live their working lives under that kind of pressure.** Most people aren't put on the spot every day, laying their tastes on the line and risking money that they have worked hard to earn.

> *So, you've got to keep your customer
> on the spot—that is, primed for the
> close—but massage him so that the
> tension that goes with being on the
> spot will be eased.*

In other words, you have to teach him a little bit of what you have had to learn in the sales profession: decisions are difficult to learn to make, but there is relief and pride when you face the music and do it!

One of the most effective closing sentences is the simple two-word phrase: "Buy it." Said with conviction, in a level tone, it suggests to the customer that you know what you're talking about, and you're sharing your good sense with him.

But you may have to try several approaches to calm those nerves.

IT'S TOO EXPENSIVE!

If the payments look formidable, you have to put them into proper perspective. The monthly cost of a family encyclopedia, say, may look fairly substantial to a young father, but you can compare it with what is already spent on something non-essential, or with what might be spent for magazines, tutors and transportation to the library. **Turn the problem of cost into an advantage by making the right type of comparison.**

DO I REALLY NEED IT?

If the product seems to represent too sudden a change in the customer's style of living, *make clear how accepted the product is* with conventional people he knows or, if you sense there is a better way to play it, *encourage him to take the risk.* Think how often you have wanted to do something but didn't, just because there wasn't a facilitator there to say, "Go ahead." You are the facilitator. You are the devil who will make him do it, a good back-up role for someone who is already sorely tempted.

MY SPOUSE MIGHT NOT LIKE IT. . .

If the customer is concerned that a spouse might not agree, you don't let them walk—you move at once. Get to the telephone and reach the other party, or have the customer do so. You are there, *right now,* to answer any questions or objections that might be raised. At worst, if you can't get the agreement of the spouse (who will certainly be caught off guard when the call is made), you can make an appointment for both to return. *But your goal is always to make the close immediately.* The script goes something like this: your spouse wants your support in a decision he's made, *not* your spouse won't buy this product unless you say so. If possible, you want to be the first to speak to the spouse, and you want to get agreement to the sale before handing the phone to your customer. "Sounds okay to me, honey," is about as fine a closing line as you could ask for.

CAN I GET A BETTER DEAL ELSEWHERE?

If the customer feels that you don't have the best deal in town, it may be too late to massage him. You probably neglected to prepare him for the close.

> *From the opening of your sales conversation to the final signing, you should be hinting, stating, repeating how advantageous your deal will be to the customer.*

After all, you are definitely giving the best deal in town. Maybe not the lowest price, or the best service contract, but in some way, which you have worked out with yourself before ever greeting a customer face-to-face, **you must have decided already what makes your deal the best.** That is the *substance* of your message. You can try to relax the customer with this information just before the close, but it is more effective if you have prepared the way. This type of massage should be employed throughout the sales pitch.

Calmed, because you are so confident that you must be trustworthy. **Eager,** because your own personal conviction has convinced him. **Massaged,** because you have found the keys to his insecurity about making the purchase, **the customer should be ready to sign.** Now, we do it.

CHAPTER SIX
Get the Signature
Then Doublecheck

You don't hesitate. You strike.

You get it all into position.

On the intellectual plane, you make sure that you have got across the facts that matter to the customer, and *only* those facts.

On the psychological plane, you sense that you have reached a peak of interest and desire. It may not be the only peak you can reach, and it may not be the highest possible, but you don't wait for Everest because, in the close, it's often true that a foot hill will do. When there's a surge, don't monitor it for energy levels, just catch that wave.

On the physical plane, you will have established some sort of contact between the two of you that is casual, warm and natural, and you will have everything prepared to make signing easy: the pen is out and the pad open, and the two materialize in front of the customer's gaze.

Make it painless!

DON'T MOVE AN INCH

If you can, have the client sitting in a comfortable chair, but not one so comfortable that sitting forward to sign a sales slip is an effort. **You want him to be able to sign without disturbing himself,** without having to move anything but his hand to form his signature.

If the two of you are standing, you manoeuvre him into a casual and comfortable position, with the pad and pencil at your elbow. If he's tall and feels at ease leaning on your glass counter, let him get into his slouch, and then slip the sales book to the edge of his extended palm. No matter how he gets comfortable when standing, you should get him to some surface that is above waist height, so that he can sign by merely turning to one side. You don't want the slightest hesitation to arise, by having the customer walk from one part of the room to another to sign, or radically alter his position. You don't want he signing to have the feel of a formal occasion. You want it to happen naturally— the obvious result of the conversation that you are having.

If you are dealing with a client in *his* home or office, you may have to sharpen your dunking skills. Note where the customer situates himself when he is most relaxed and expansive. Does he lean back in his chair, putting his hands behind his head, or does he hunch forward, putting his elbows on his desk? Whatever the position that indicates that he is relaxed and open to suggestion, you must slip your book to a place that will take advantage of that position. *Pounce.* If he's happy lying back in a recliner, aim your sales book for his belly button and slip it over, holding it for him to take. You'll get the hang of it, if you remember the main point: **The most natural position is the one that advances your cause.** The position is a reflection of mood, and, conversely, a forced change in position to sign a sales slip might produce a constricted mood.

When you've got him where you want him, get him! And if he balks, wait until he gets there again. And again. **To get the signature, you keep asking for the signature.**

DON'T LET PAYMENT POSTPONE THE CLOSE

Is a deposit required? Before you ask for the signature, you must be very clear about what is the minimum you can take and still feel adequately protected. **Don't give a vague guestimate;** write down, as you talk, the two specific figures: the amount you prefer to get, the least amount you can go with. And stick to them.

Unfortunately, the deposit can give a customer an excuse, if he's wavering, to come back another day. He doesn't have the money with him, or his cheque won't clear at the bank—that kind of thing.

Don't let yourself get backed into that particular corner. You can take a post-dated cheque, for example. You can walk around the corner with him to his bank or an automatic money machne. You can call the boss and ask that the deposit be lowered (a dangerous move, unless necessary, because the customer is being given a break from the sustained force of your sales presentation). You can even take out your wallet—if the amount is small enough or you are dramatic enough—and offer to lay down the deposit yourself.

What do all these stratagems say to the customer? That you are *determined* to make the sale at that moment, no matter what the minor obstacles he or his situation present. Such determination is an argument in itself. **He will be won over by the steady beat of your intent.** What do these ploys do for the close? They emphasize that it is important to act promptly, ignoring the petty details as much as possible. **They show that it is the sale that is important, not the sales arrangement.** They help both you and the customer concentrate on the matter at hand.

Your goal:

> *Don't let the* **need** *for a deposit become a customer's* **excuse** *for delay. Try every reasonable method of getting* something, *so the commitment will be ratified.*

A close is a goal, and closing is the end of the game, but, as we are about to see, you've got to take some control of the future, just as you've controlled the steps leading up to the close.

Doublecheck Everything!

Everything. From your end, and from the customer's end, as well.

You want to be certain that your product is delivered, that it works and continues to work, that the customer is satisfied, that he knows how to contact you if there should be a problem.

On the other hand, you want to be equally certain that no problems will come down on your head because the customer has not been straight with you about a credit reference or has honestly misunderstood just what the sale means to him.

Get the Signature Then Doublecheck

You have a lot to remember as you manoeuvre the customer toward the sale, but you must not put these aspects on the back burner—or you get burned.

HIGH HOPES

Even as you are touting the merits of a product and downplaying its negative aspects, **you must tell your sales story so clearly that no false expectations are raised. Listen to the customer listening to you.** Does he *understand* that the television set will not make coffee in the morning? Does he realize that horizontal stripes are not going to make his waist look svelte? Does he understand that typewriters need ribbon replacements and portable tape recorders may require new batteries every ten hours of play, and so forth?

You have nothing to gain, and much to lose, by letting the customer have false expectations. He isn't taking shorthand notes of the conversation. He won't remember what you said, word for word, and what he imagined you said, and what he simply made up—these will all be melded together into one impression of the whole sales encounter. It's your responsibility—and a very difficult one—to get the picture clear and in focus.

*And you must be confident in your
sales powers without becoming
overconfident.*

The close you work so hard to make must be airtight

and sound. What you promise, you must deliver.

THE BUCK STOPS HERE.

If there's going to be any deviation, whatever the reason, whoever's really at fault, you have to jump on it and solve the problem beforehand. Make sure that the warehouse informs you if, for any reason, a promised delivery will be delayed. You, of course, dash to the telephone and **deal with the customer yourself.** The responsibility is yours! **The buck stops with you.** You don't chicken out.

Of course, you cannot prevent mistakes that are made by someone else in your organization. But you are the customer's only point of contact with that organization. You are his advocate when there is a problem—an ombudsman, because that is your side of the commitment.

CLEAR AND ACCURATE

It is also your responsibility to see that the paperwork is accurate, in every respect. You've done it a thousand times? Well, that's when you begin to make mistakes. Everyone in business knows the value of checking and double-checking and re-checking again. You may have been distracted as you were computing the sales tax. You can easily transpose a couple of digits in the stock number; people often do. Your writing might be misleading to someone who isn't familiar with your handwriting style.

Check what you've done, or have someone else do it. A fresh eye will see what you pass over. **And check**

procedures where necessary. Has the delivery schedule been changed while you were away on vacation, or has the business office decided to increase or decrease the interest charged to the unpaid balance in credit accounts? Sometimes people you work with will forget to pass along the most obvious information, because they take it for granted. **Always keep on top of current procedures,** in particular as they affect your customers.

OUT OF STOCK

And, of course, you must never be caught out on the out-of-stock problem.

Few things are more damaging than the successful close that is then followed by an unexpected three months delay for delivery. The point of your power sell is to get the customer to want the product immediately. If you are successful, and then your own mistake leads to disappointment because you didn't check the stock recently enough, the success will turn to ashes in your mouth. The customer will lose respect for you and perhaps feel deceived, no matter what you protest. The bitter word will be passed around.

Worse, you will really have done someone a *disservice.* By the time the product finally arrives, it will no longer bring as much pleasure as it would have in the beginning. Your job—to bring people pleasure and benefit—has not been done.

But not every complaint from a customer will be as legitimate as this one. As we will see, there is a large family of gripes.

CHAPTER SEVEN
Legitimate Complaints versus Griping

Legitimate Complaints versus Griping

There are two families of complaints that you will have to deal with after a sale: the legitimate ones and the gripes. You want to act upon the former immediately; solving such problems is essential to your self-respect as a sales professional.

As for gripes, you will have to be careful in making the distinction, and you will have to remember the virtues of extreme patience. As we have noted elsewhere in this book, there is at least one inviolable rule in selling:

The customer is indeed always right.

That doesn't mean that you will always replace a product, when the complaint is really only a gripe, but it does mean that you will try to satisfy the customer on every other possible score: the sympathy with which you listen, the alternative avenues of solving the problem that you can suggest, the diversion of the dissatisfaction to more productive areas.

Remember:

The griper is not necessarily trying to deceive you.

He may think that the gripe is a legitimate complaint; your first approach is to help him understand the difference. He may not even be in control of his gripe. It might be a displacement from some problem elsewhere in his life. He may think he's unhappy with the new curtains in the living room when he's really unhappy with the neighbours who live across the street. Sometimes, someone with a gripe is only looking for a sympathetic ear. You can supply that always, as part of customer service.

Take a look at some examples:

LEGITIMATE: *IT DOESN'T WORK*

If it doesn't work, fix it—unless it has been unreasonably abused or has lasted long past the average life of the product. If someone buys a product to perform a task, he has a right to demand that the product perform the task. **That's fair.** And you have the responsibility, as we've already suggested, to ensure that the complaint is answered.

GRIPE: *WE DON'T LIKE IT*

Sad, but not your fault. If the product is what you showed or described, does what it is supposed to (and doesn't frighten the children or leak on the rug), it's not your responsibility that it gives the customer no pleasure. You can wonder what went wrong, because you have something to learn. You can, and should, concentrate on helping the customer deal with this gripe and return to the good feelings he had at the close. Were his expectations too high? Have his tastes changed? Is he responding to criticisms from friends and family members? You are not able to do anything about such problems, but you can try to give him the courage to trust his original feelings. You tapped into something real in him when you made the close; try to get him to remember what it was.

LEGITIMATE: *YOUR NEW PRODUCT MAKES IT OBSOLETE, AND I WASN'T WARNED*

Maybe a little iffy, in certain situations, but this customer may have a justified complaint, even if you didn't know about the new product yourself.

The right answer will depend upon the situation. If someone has made a major investment in electronic equipment, perhaps you and the company should work out some very attractive trade-in terms. Even if you or your firm did not mean to deceive, you have placed the customer in a position that is not as advantageous as he was led to expect at the close.

GRIPE: *THE COLOUR'S WRONG*

We're all adults here. Both you and the customer had the shared responsibility of making this and similar decisions *before* the close. Of course, if the product is delivered, and an honest mistake has been made, it is reasonable to exchange the product for one of another colour. A colour under showroom lights might look very different in the home.

But if the customer has waited several weeks after delivery to decide that the colour is wrong, he is just griping. Handle as you would any other gripe.

GRIPE: *MY SPOUSE DOESN'T LIKE IT*

We are all adults, and the closing of the sale was an act
that took place between consenting adults. You are always wise to bring up the possible response of a spouse,
but you are not obliged to do so.

If the sale is minor and you expect to continue business with the customer over the years, you may want to
make an exchange. Company policy, of course, will
play a part in your decision. The bottom line, though,
is recourse to your own sales intuition. Is the customer
using the spouse as a cover for their own change of
heart? Have they had the product—and presumably
used it—for a considerable period of time? Are they,
in short, really playing fair with you?

LEGITIMATE (SOMETIMES): *IT HASN'T STOOD UP TO WEAR.*

But how much wear? You can avoid this type of complaint—most of the time—if you are careful to find out
how your product is going to be used. You can always
stick by the manufacturer's promise, but that is a happy
medium, in the best of all possible worlds. You have a
responsibility to learn exactly what your customer demands of a product before letting it out of the store.
You can't prevent a customer from buying a suite of an-
tique walnut furniture for use beside the pool, but you
should make sure that you both understand what future
lies in wait for the purchase—and that the customer is

Legitimate Complaints versus Griping

clearly, unforgettably warned.

On the other hand, the product may be defective.

You have to use judgement, based upon your reading of the customer and your knowledge of the product. If too many customers begin calling with this kind of complaint, it may be time for you to consider selling another product—or bring renewed clarity to your sales presentation.

In any event, one way to forestall complaints and other forms of customer unhappiness is to study your customer's style of living and style of behaviour. The life that he leads with your product is pretty much out of control, but you should do your best to start it off on the right foot, as we see next.

CHAPTER EIGHT
Knowing Your Customer's Style

Knowing Your Customer's Style

One way to avoid problems after the close is to learn all you can about your customer's style of living. Don't make assumptions, based upon what the product offers or upon what other customers have done with the product.

In other words, you must add an extra dimension to your *reading* of a customer while you are trying to divine his tastes and desires. That's the main part of the job, and it will lead you to a successful close. **The extra dimension comes in speculating about the life he and the product will have with each other.**

Just because the customer wants a vintage sports car, and you have determined through your own analysis that he is particularly attracted to the style and quirkiness of a Morgan, for example, that doesn't mean that your job of using customer insight is done.

Yes, you've found out what he wanted, and you have found what he can use, but you haven't found out what he can take care of, necessarily.

In this case, you may mention the necessity of tuning up the engine frequently, or of paying particular attention to the chassis (which is made of wood), and, to an extent, he may hear you. You *may* be satisfied that he got the message. But it's still not unlikely that he will appear on your doorstep within the next few months, steaming at the inconveniences he has endured because of this sports car's special demands.

From your experience, you have to speculate: *Does he understand what he's getting into?* Will he be able to maintain the car so that it can do what it's supposed to, and continue to give the pleasure he's seeking?

- You can't hold his hand, but you can prevent a situation that will get out of hand.
- You want to make a sale, but you don't want to set in motion a series of unpleasant encounters.
- If you see a potential problem that he doesn't see, you should make him see it.

There is a type of customer that always buys the coloured chicken at Easter, or the turtle with the decal on its back, and doesn't realize that such creatures have to eat and drink, have to be kept warm, have the odd habit (if they don't die of inattention first) of growing older and larger and smellier.

In a very special sense, **you have to know that your product will have a good home.** You have to know that it won't pose a danger to a houseful of young children, that it will be given the maintenance it needs, that it will not be subjected to unusual abuse.

> *Knowing your customer's style of living will help you predict possible problems.*

You can save them from themselves, if that is necessary.

But perhaps this is sounding too negative. On the contrary, you can perform a *real* service, and something of a rare one, by helping the customer change his style to suit the product that he really wants.

Let's say that you can perceive that he will never—no

matter how much he protests and how eagerly he means it—really get into the habit of properly servicing his sports car on a regular basis. The positive approach is to work out a system. Perhaps you arrange for him to be called and serviced by a good mechanic—at his own expense, of course. Perhaps, when the item is important enough, you will call him every six months or so and ask him *specifically* whether or not he has seen to the obligatory tune-up.

If someone with a herd of rough and tumbling children has their heart set on a Ming vase, you can discuss how to arrange their house and change the traffic patterns there, so as to give the art object protection. **In other words, the positive approach may involve several ounces of prevention.** It is not the product that has to be saved in such situations, although there is something almost unforgivable about waste of a finely made object. Still, the real aim is to save the relationship the customer has established with the product. You want to have *customer satisfaction,* and that comes from a long and happy life for the product.

A more subtle aspect of style, and a very touchy one, is whether or not the customer will be able to *sell* the product to his friends and family members. You can rarely bring this problem up, unless the customer does himself, but you should be aware of the potential for disaster. As we suggested in an earlier chapter, you don't want the customer to be subjected to ridicule, even if the taste you are selling him is *objectively* superior in every way to the products that his friends buy.

The new product has to fit into the family, just like a new spouse with in-laws. It has to fit into the everyday life of the customer.

If you point out the possible difficulties on this score, don't *insist* upon them. **The customer, in the final analysis, will decide.** If things go a bit sour, they will remember that you warned them, in a sense. That makes you their ally. You and they still believe in the product, and that may help them stick to their original convictions about it.

But when your best and strongest efforts seem to come a cropper, do you start making a list of your failures? Not if you have the power to sell, you don't. As we shall see, there is an up side to the down side of every sales experience.

CHAPTER NINE
Salvaging What You Can

Salvaging What You Can

There are many things that can happen and turn a successful close into a sour deal. Here are just a few:

- You have to take the product back, because the complaint turned out to be undeniably legitimate.
- You didn't take a product back after a gripe, but the ensuing *scene* left a cloud over your entire week.
- You thought a product would be ideal for a certain customer, and you hear through the grapevine that he actually detests it.
- You thought you were giving the best deal around on a certain item, and you discover that there's a much better deal available from a store on the other side of town.

Well, now's the time for a little philosophy, just as you suspect. Mistakes have the virtue of being tremendous educational resources. What do you think happened to sour the sale? Was someone at fault, or did the Fates just work against you and your customer? How can similar problems be prevented in the future?

There are several things you are likely to learn.

They're simple.

They're important.

PEOPLE ARE RATIONAL

If a complaint turns into accusations that lead to a shouting-match, no one is going to be edified. But if you step back a bit when you first receive the complaint, **let the customer spout off steam**—which has been building, maybe, because he really didn't have the nerve to make a call until he was livid—then you have returned to the power position.

He'll be a little sheepish, particularly if you agree with his justified complaint, or with the source of his feeling when he actually only has a gripe. He'll see that you're trying to be fair; he wants to be fair, too. Most of the time, a customer builds up an almost demonic image of you and your company, when things go wrong. You were so much in control of the sales encounter, you knew your job cold—so how could *this* happen? *You* must have planned it. *You must have known it would happen.*

That's an irrational reaction, of course, and irrational reactions result in irrational behaviour. **You don't walk away, but you let things cool off.** The customer is under a version of the pressure he felt during the close. He has seen his money wasted—just as he had feared all along, before you began massaging his fears and insecurities. He feels, at some level of consciousness, that he has been duped—and the *facts* seem to bear him out.

But if you let him cool off, if you bring the rational approach to bear in your handling of the complaint— above all, if you never let your voice reveal the slightest sign of anger or disbelief—then you will benefit from his mood swing. His great anger will be followed by relief. He's got it off his chest. Now, he will be ready to listen to what you propose—so long as you keep cool and convince him that you're still on his side, even if his call is a gripe and not a legitimate complaint.

If you're fair, people will be fair. That's the given, or it's time to put ourselves in separate soundproof cells and concentrate on our navels.

YOU'RE STRONGER THAN YOU THINK

Yes, you knew you were persuasive, but you didn't know that a customer would trust you so much that he is dumbfounded when your product or service seems to fail.

You're better than you think. **But you are also using powers of salesmanship that should be carefully controlled.** If you have become so convinced of your own position that you are unconsciously intimidating people into making decisions that are not right for them and their life situations, perhaps it's time to reassess your approach. Like any force, your powers in selling can be overreaching. You want to be able to convince people, persuade them, *sell* them, but you do not want to have too much impact.

YOU DON'T QUITE KNOW YOUR PRODUCT

Perhaps you're letting the product get into the *wrong* hands, if several people are having difficulty with it. Perhaps you and they expect too much of it, or don't understand one of its complexities.

If you get the feeling that something is going wrong all too frequently, it's time to do some product research of your own. Call around to the customers who have *not* complained. Why are they happy? What are the things they like best, and what has not been as pleasing as they had hoped when you closed with them?

When you get a picture of how your product is actually used, of who actually derives the most benefit from it, you will be better prepared to focus on customers in the future. Your research will help you anticipate problems, as well as give you more expertise in determining who will really be happy with what they bought from you.

A NEW SERVICE MIGHT BE NECESSARY.

From dealing with complaints, you should begin to get an idea of what the community really wants. Perhaps it's time for your firm to consider instituting a new type of service. Perhaps you should be looking at new products to represent. Sometimes, you might even have an idea for an improvement to your product that will make it more attractive to the customers you serve.

Be creative. See how there can be an opportunity in what seems, at first, to be merely unpleasantness. **Finding out what went wrong** will give you added strength, because you can sharpen your attack upon potential problems in the most direct and effective way. **Dealing with people** who have complaints or gripes and giving them the satisfaction they deserve will be personally beneficial to you, because you will have even more positive feelings about yourself and your skills as a power seller. **Anticipating problems** for the future will increase your control over the individual sales encounter and will give more clarity to the shape of your career in sales.

Coming up with answers is what you want to do, because you want to be the person who solves problems. You do not want to evade, or make excuses, or change the grounds upon which an agreement has been reached.

Most of all, your intention is to ensure that a **closed sale remains closed,** if that is humanly possible. You have created a minor emotional and intellectual climax in the customer's life, when you brought him to the pitch required to sign on the dotted line. You and he both have invested much of yourselves in achieving that moment; it was indeed a shared achievement.

Any disappointments that follow should be shared, as well. That is your responsibility, even if it is a demanding one. You will increase your selling powers immeasurably if you meet the challenges that follow a close as vigorously as you face those presented by the initial sale.

AFTERWORD

Conclusion

Let's review:

Power closing is the most critical goal of power selling. Everything else, no matter how well and creatively you bring it off, literally has no meaning if you cannot move the customer from fever pitch to the dotted line.

And of all the skills you have developed, and continue to develop, you can never afford to lose the ability to

- Know when it's time to close.
- Know how to make the close happen.
- Ensure that the close sticks.

These abilities will be the one you have to practice from now until the end of your sales career.

Look around at the veterans in the field. Watch how they bring a sale to a close. Ask how they bring a sale to close.

Jot down the words or phrases that, typically, they use when they have decided to strike. If you ask them for such phrases and they claim not to have any, that's not because they don't want to help you but because such phrases become ingrained, almost automatic. But every expert sales professional has developed a set of key phrases that signal the coming of the close. Sooner, and not later, you will find the ones that suit your personal style. They let you know that you have arrived at a critical point in the sales encounter.

Don't ever take "no" for the *final* answer. You accept it every time, acceding to the customer's feelings at that moment, but you come back to the closing questions again and again until the signature is on the sales slip or contract and the financial commitment has been made.

It's good to remember the obvious things:

- A sale is not a sale unless money is committed to the enterprise.
- The only proof positive of your work is the accumulation of signatures; all of the rest gets dispersed into the air.
- You judge your work by the number of closes you make.
- A promise to return, to consider, to spread the word will, if you add a quarter, get you three minutes on a public telephone.
- Promises are not sales; commitments are.

Why is the closing considered the hardest part of Power Selling?

It's the climax, the summation of everything you've done before that critical moment.

In itself, the closing is just a phrase or two, but the *impact* of that phrase is a function of the power you've streamed into the sales encounter from the beginning. This is the high note. But you don't get to it until you've set out the theme, worked it over in the development and repetition, and begun your build to the climax.

It is also the most exciting moment in the sales encounter, the moment when you get the bull's ears and his tail, or nothing. You should yearn for this moment

Conclusion

of challenge, because the desire to make a tremendous success as a salesperson is coursing through your blood. *Each closing should make you want to make another.* You should become a connoisseur of closings: This one, you took too fast; that one, you felt a lot of bumps along the way; the next one, you soared straight to the goal. Become a connoisseur, and enjoy the different shapes and moods that accompany each individual close; but don't forget that **the point is the *result*.** A name on a piece of paper.

And if you have to remind your customer too often of what the game is about, perhaps you need to remind yourself. You are in sales, and you are proud of it.

You can help people, and you can build an enviable, profitable career. You contribute to the growth of the nation's economy, and you are able to exercise all of the talents, gifts and yearnings that define you as an individual.

Selling gives you the opportunity to feel the muscle of your mental intellectual and emotional powers. It challenges you at every level of human experience.

And it's a hell of a lot of fun.

When are you going to make your next close?

PART FIVE: PERSONAL POWER SELL

INTRODUCTION TO PART FIVE

Introduction to Part Five

Here's a strange statistic: **Many people in sales spend no more than a quarter of their work time actually talking face-to-face with customers.**

What are they doing the rest of the time? Writing up orders? Not if so little of their time is spent dealing with prospects eyeball-to-eyeball.

Are they spending the other three quarters of the working day chasing down prospects, manning the telephone or mailing out teasers to bring in customers? If they are, they're doing something wrong, because you don't spend background time at the ratio of three-to-one and make decent money in sales.

The power in Power Selling comes from the realization of your personal potential. You stoke up that power, in preparation for the test—actual encounters with prospects you mean to change into customers. If you aren't having those encounters, **if you're spending more than half your time trying to arrange those encounters, you're wasting your most important resource:** your personal power in commanding the dynamics of the sales situation.

Remember the true focus of your sales career, the excitement that drew you to this line of work in the first place: It's the test of your skills in the unpredictable, difficult and ultimately rewarding one-on-one sales discussion.

Sure, you get tired some days, and even the most successful salespersons become discouraged on occasion. *But what brings you back to your feet, ready to hit the sales floor or the sales circuit again?* What sets the adrenalin flowing? It's the desire—if you're the kind of salesperson who firmly believes in their own power as a professional in sales—to match yourself against the problems that lie between you and a potential customer. There might be the obstacle of cost. . .or the fear of trying something new. . .or the possibility of opposition at home . . . or some basic—and unexpressed—inability to come to a decision. These problems, and a thousand others, require your attention. Clear them away, and the customer will be ready to buy. One source of your power in controlling sales encounters is that you *know* they want to buy. . .and it's your goal to release them from whatever chains of doubt and self-doubt are keeping from moving to the fulfillment of their desire.

In this book, we'll be talking about:

- The nine basic power streams to successful selling
- The difference between radiating confidence and coming off as a con
- How to listen to the customer
- How to lay your attitude upon the customer
- How to "read" the customer to find out what makes him tick
- How to be as diplomatic as the Swiss, when something misfires between you and the customer on the personal level.

And there will also be some pointers on *preparation*. Do you have to wait until you see the client before you begin taking charge of his attitudes? What's the value of paperwork? What's the sure method of making your impact felt over the telephone? Just how important is follow-up? *We have some of the clues, but you will have to supply the individuality of approach that is the key to your own personal power.*

> *You begin by deciding that today you are going to up the percentage of your working day that involves direct contact with customers.*

Take a look at yourself, an honest look. Figure up precisely just how much time you spend in active sales conversations with live prospects. Don't guess; a guess is based on self-deception. Figure it out in black-and-white. If the answer is less than 30%, set yourself a goal of 40% by the end of the month, and 50% by the end of next month.

What's the optimum? That will depend upon the type of sales you do. A better question is: **Is what I do when I'm not face-to-face with a customer essential to my career? Does it have to take so much of my day?** Find out how much time you could devote to pesonal contact, at the maximum. Write that down in terms of actual minutes and hours. And then add 20% to it.

Yes, this is a book with a definite point of view:

> *You should be working to the limit of your power potential, and the power potential of a salesperson is explosively realized in the eyeball-to-eyeball sales encounter.*

CHAPTER ONE
Confidence versus the "Con" Man

Confidence versus the "Con" Man

If you really can't make a silk purse out of a sow's ear, you certainly can't turn a con artist into a sincere, warm, thoughtful representative of the sales profession (at least not with one little book on power selling).

But we're not talking about dyed-in-the-wool rip-off artists; we're talking about you and the hundreds of thousands of men and women all across the country who know that sales work is important and helpful, as well as potentially profitable and personally fulfilling. *We're talking about an honourable profession that sometimes gets a bad name because of a few less-than-honourable individuals*, and we're talking about the bad deal you might get sometimes, before you even begin

There's something else, too. Just as some people have the wrong idea about salespeople, some people starting out in sales have a similarly wrong idea: they think they have to come on strong, bully or bedazzle the customer, cut corners to make a deal, and come off carrying a trophy, to show that they're tough.

That kind of approach is not based upon the Power Sell concept; it's just a kind of "con," and it doesn't get you very far. On the contrary, after you've been in the profession a few years, you'll discover—it's really true—that customers and colleagues alike will stay away from the con artist. The smell is unmistakable.

But *confidence* is something else again: self-assurance rather than self-satisfaction. Confidence is based upon competence, and it is augmented by conviction, and it is expressed in co-operation. **Competence, conviction, co-operation:** Let's see how those three ideas build into that critical manifestation of personal selling power—**true confidence.**

COMPETENCE

Yes, there's no way around it. You have to do your homework before you can really feel the confidence that will give you power to win customers to your point of view.

It's not just a matter of knowing product specs, or competitors' prices—although that is important information. It's not just knowing how your product works; in fact, many successful salespeople think that it's a waste of time to know too much about the inner workings or theoretical underpinnings of a product—the customer who cares about such things probably knows them already, and discussion of them distracts from the main goal: the signature on the sales slip.

Competence is a broader concept.

It's knowing in advance, for example, what questions the customer is likely to ask. Perhaps you will have to get the help of your peers in finding this out, and there's certainly something to be said for a *minimum* of idle gossip with your fellow salespersons. You can pick up good hints this way. However you do it, you have to *anticipate* what someone in your town today is going to have on his mind when he confronts your product.

Confidence versus the "Con" Man

Competence is also knowing in detail how the mechanics of the sale will affect the customer. Some salespersons like to affect a blithe ignorance of such matters as billing procedures and delivery dates. This will undercut your image of competence, and it won't make a customer eager to deal with you again, because we're talking about those things that become important to him *after* the sale.

Know about billing dates, interest costs, credit checks and related matters so that you can answer accurately and immediately. Don't, for example, fire up a customer's eagerness to buy an expensive set of furniture, fill his head with visions of comfort and style, get him to sign and *then* "discover" that delivery won't be possible for several months. Know what you can offer in *every* aspect of the sales process, not just in terms of the product itself.

Competence is also knowing whether or not the product or service is going to satisfy your customer in the long run. That's tricky, and we don't recommend refusing to sell to someone who's eager to buy, but there's a thin line here: Make a mistake and sell the wrong thing, and the word may get out that you're the type who sells refrigerators to Eskimos. Sound good? Not when you realize that you're dealing with people who see you as a victimizer.

What springs from competence?
Self-confidence.

And it will fairly radiate from your pores as you face a customer. No one ever has to announce that he feels self-confident. It shows. And so does competence, when you are prepared to answer the problems that concern your customers.

CONVICTION

You can't fake conviction. In fact, you can't really fake any emotion and be a sales professional in the Power Sell mould.

*You have to believe. There's no way
around it.*

You have to believe that your product is the best possible. If it's not, then you have to believe that it's a good deal, even considering its weaknesses, for the customers you serve. And if it's not so remarkable a product, then you can believe, if it's true, that at least it brings some pleasure or relief to people who can't afford anything better.

Those are possible beliefs, if they can be based on truth. If you can't find conviction, real honest-to-God, down-to-the-bone conviction, in support of your service or product, you can become a con artist (but we've already discarded that possibility), or you can find another product to sell.

You don't have to believe that your product is 24-

carat gold. Few are. But if its 18 carat, you have to have the conviction that it offers certain advantages that are real and useful to your customers.

What is the most important service provided by your product? Is it efficiency or savings, longevity or dependability? Write down the answers in your own terms, not in the words of the ad department. What about the psychology involved? You know your customers. Do they like your product because it makes them one of the crowd, or because it helps bring the family closer together, or because it testifies to financial success?

Write down the answer. In those answers will lie the source of your conviction about the value of the product. When you walk confidently to your next prospect, you will be secure in your knowledge. You'll know what's good about the product, where you put your trust, and where you can honestly suggest that others place their trust.

If you have conviction, you don't have to waste energy in devising arguments. You know them, because you believe them. You just speak from inner conviction.

CO-OPERATION

There's the traditional image of the con artist virtually launching an assault on the hapless customer, who buys as a gesture of surrender.

A confident salesperson, on the other hand, engages

in a co-operative act with the customer. Because of the *competence* he's earned and the *conviction* he's found on his own, he feels self-confident enough to use his powers, not abuse them. He presents the case for his product to the customer. Because of the *competence* he's earned and the *conviction* he's found on his own, he feels self-confident enough to use his powers, not abuse them. He presents the case for his product to the customer. He invites the customer to become involved in the assessment of the product.

You can see how confidence makes it unnecessary for any salesperson to shower the customer with inflated claims or suggest that a good deal is really a steal.

If you have confidence, you can co-operate, because you feel secure about your side of the negotiation, secure enough to reach across the divide and help your interlocutor with his decision.

If you have confidence based upon competence, you know that you will never be caught out. You will be delivering the goods, in every sense of the expression, because you know your job. You will have justifiable pride—something all too few people these days can say about their job.

If you have confidence grounded in conviction, you know that everything you say will come across clearly and credibly.

*If you're convinced, other people
will be convinced.*

Condidence versus the "Con" Man

You will see that your powers as a successful sales professional will increase tremendously, growing from each encounter with a customer, if you make sure that your confidence is not a pose but **the real thing:** a product of competence, conviction and the ability to approach the customer in a co-operative spirit.

But co-operation is impossible if you're listening only to yourself. You have to hear even as you are heard, as we see next.

CHAPTER TWO
Hearing versus Listening

Hearing versus Listening

Another misconception: The salesperson sure of his powers will talk a customer's ear off. He will answer every objection, forestall any quibbling and rush the customer on a wall of sound to the close.

Wrong.

Today, at any rate, the customer is too informed about consumer issues, too well educated and too independent to stand still for the wall of sound. It would be a barrier between you and the sale.

We have been through some tough times economically in recent years. Even people who may not have much of a formal education are very well educated by experience to some harsh realities. They know that the economy can slide, that interest rates can rise, that life's savings and farms and second homes can be lost overnight. They have seen what unsettlement in the world economy can mean to the average consumer. In short, they have learned to be careful with their money. They want things to be reasonably priced and efficient. They want to believe that many purchases can be seen as investments. **They want to spend money wisely.**

There are other factors in the land, as well. Some people may have developed the idea that foreign-made goods are superior—or, conversely, that such goods are unfair competition. Some people are hoping to buy into a certain social class, or style of living, by making the appropriate purchases. More and more people are hoping that they can buy a good life for their children, who may be "only" children with high expectations placed upon them. Other people are concerned about product safety, or about the labour practices of a product manufacturer.

Which of these matters do you bring up? How do you know which ones matter to the customer?

No problem—*if* you know how to listen.

> *You bring up only those aspects*
> *of a product that are of interest*
> *to the customer.*

Everything else is irrelevant at best and, at worst, distracting.

To find out what aspects *are* important, you listen.

Sounds simple? The truth is, most people in your profession have never learned how to listen actively rather than passively. They will *hear*, if the customer makes a point, but they rarely *listen*, to see if there may be the half-said, or the unspoken, or the confused thought in the air, blocking acceptance of the product.

LISTENING IS WATCHING

Does someone look you straight in the eye? Do they have nervous movements? Do they lower their voice, as in embarrassment or conspiracy, or look to the side as they speak?

Any visual clues you catch are important in letting you in on the true meaning behind the spoken word. You have to separate the nervousness some people feel in any one-to-one encounter from other kinds of nervousness—for example, about the price, or about whether the style is too "young." The body language of the customer will give away his inner feelings.

LISTENING IS LEADING

When you catch a clue, pick up on it, and run with it. Find out quickly if your guess is right.

Have you perceived that price is bothering the customer? Talk about it, see if the discussion calms him down, lead into more productive and positive ways of considering the price angle.

Whatever you think you've learned from your listening, put it to proof right away. Even in extreme emotional episodes, we sometimes can't tell whether someone is laughing hysterically or weeping uncontrollably, unless we have other clues. You will not always "read" the customer's unspoken thoughts with accuracy, but you keep trying, keeping your ear on the alert.

LISTENING IS WAITING

Some people aren't able to express themselves clearly, particularly when they are pressuring themselves about a possible sales decision. Their imprecision of language reveals their own uncertainty, and their inexperience, in many cases, in dealing verbally with a stranger.

You are to use your selling power to give momentum to the sales conversation; that is basic. *But you must never roll over the customer, or seem obviously to rush him.* If he doesn't make himself clear, you let him try again.

> **Your goal is to get him to the point where he says, "Yes, I want to buy."**

Can you hear that thought in some other half-focused sentence? Often you can. Suppose the customer says, "My daughter sure would like having that around" and goes on talking. You should bring them back around to the daughter again, in a few moments, because that might be the key. Actually, he was on the verge of agreeing to buy, but backed off.

You have to hear the surge of interest that often comes to the tip of the tongue, associated with some other factor, so that you can work on bringing it all the way to the surface.

LISTENING IS TOUCHING

You can develop the ability to "listen" through your fingers. When you move someone toward the product with a light touch on the shoulder, when you shake someone's hand or when you hand them a folder or the product itself, you can "read" whether or not they have relaxed with you.

You never want to push people around or touch people who obviously don't like being touched—a very useful clue—but you can often bring the customer closer to a sale by instilling a calm, relaxed atmosphere. A confident handshake, but not a bone-crusher...a gentle hand on the shoulder, but not a backslap —such simple, warm gestures, when used with taste and good sense, can transmit some of your self-confidence to the customer.

You don't have to believe in some kind mystical transference, but you will see that it works. Your self-confident vibes will have their effect.

LISTENING IS IMAGINING

You have to be careful, because false assumptions will take you way off base; but, between the words, **a skilled and sensitive listener can imagine some very useful information.**

From what the customer says, can you imagine their family situation, their house, the car they drive, their dissatisfactions, their hopes, their tastes? You don't want to bring your guesses out in the open, unless you are very sure of two things: that you are correct, and that you won't open a can or worms. Make assumptions about someone, and they're likely to feel belittled, as if you've dismissed them as a stereotype.

The truth, of course, is that we may not be stereotypes, but we all fit patterns of living. With care and sensitivity, you can imagine the pattern of life *probably* lived by your customer, and that will give you good ideas to pursue in your sales conversation.

You don't say, "You're a blue-collar worker so I

guess you'll like this estate car because there's a lot of room in the back for cases of beer and there's a hook on the rear-view mirror for hanging a pair of furry dice."

You might say, after you've creatively imagined that what you're hearing could suggest that your customer likes dogs, that many animal-lovers have been happy with your rugs because they have been treated to resist stains.

If you strike out, drop it. But if you become a good listener, you will rarely strike out. What we really care about is never very far from the surface of our words. Most importantly, the consideration that is driving your customer when he looks over your product is right there in his thoughts. Creative listening can home in on it.

In sum:

*You have to listen more
than you talk.*

This is a hard thing to do, particularly if you're nervous with a customer—but you won't be! Few things require more self-confidence than the ability to handle a moment of silence. To let some thoughts sink in. To give the customer time to organize his own thoughts.

You have to be so confidently in control of yourself that you can listen to the silence, as you have listened to the customer. Your words will take care of themselves, because you are prepared. You don't have to be thinking about what you'll say next; you should be lis-

tening-in-depth, so you'll know how to move the customer into position.

And part of that effort, as we see now, is devoted to
bringing the two of you into the same attitude
frame. . . .

CHAPTER THREE
Infectious Attitude

Infectious Attitude

Do you bounce over to the customer on a grey day, grinning like Christmas tree lights and jolly him up? That's one way to change someone's attitude, but we suspect that people won't go from depression to good cheer; they are more likely to switch from mild interest in your product to sincere concern about the state of your mental health.

We want you to be confident, with a positive attitude. We want you to bring the customer to your level of confidence and positivity, because when you both meet there, the sale is on. But it's a rare customer these days who wants the clown act. And why start with the climax? You don't tell the customer that they have good reason to be dancing around the room when they've just stepped in out of a snowstorm or spent the morning negotiating a traffic jam.

*Your assignment: to bring him the
news and arguments that will
actually alter his mood, because he
will be getting something he needs
and wants.*

INFECTION STARTS WITH A GERM

What attitude do you want your customer to have? You have to decide, based largely upon the product and upon your own analysis of the product. Giddiness is an unlikely goal if you are dealing in burial plots; and sober analysis of durability, say, is not going to be very useful when you're trying to get someone in the mood to buy frivolous undergarments.

Look at the atmosphere of the salesroom. You may have become so accustomed to it that you don't recognize it consciously. What does it say about the product, and what mood is it likely to provoke in most customers? If you're not in a position to change the working ambience, you have to consider it as a given when you decide how you want your customer to feel just before he decides to buy.

What moods do you project best, and most honestly, in line with your feelings about yourself and your beliefs about the product? Would a purchase of this product make you excited, or give you a feeling of security, or invoke feelings of pride—or some combination of these and other feelings?

*Once you decide what a purchaser
is likely to feel when he's made the
decision to buy, then you know what
mood you're aiming for when a
prospect comes in off the street.*

You can't be infectious until you decide which infection you want to spread!

INFECTION OVERCOMES RESISTANCE

Turn on the emotion full blast, and the customer is fully prepared to resist. When you wave a flag, giving your strategy away, you are in danger of losing the whole game.

First, you have to start somewhere near the customer's mood level. Get into bed with them, in emotional terms. If they're dour, you pitch your mood down very far, but just a few points on the register above them. You have to get close, but not so close that you become infected with their low feelings. You're going to rise to where you want to go, moodwise, leading them bit by bit, always staying just a little ahead of them.

On the other hand, if someone pops in laughing heartily, they are unlikely to be ready to make a big-ticket purchase unless they're a rich eccentric out of the old movies. More likely, they are feeling jolly from a three-martini lunch, or have just had a good day and are feeling expansive. You've got to meet this person's mood partway, stopping a few points *below* it, because you want to begin the subtle task of bringing their mood down to something more serious.

Whatever the case, you are in control of the infectious act. Knowing your goal, recognizing the initial mood of the customer, you have to bring the latter to meet the former.

INFECTION SHOULD BE SYSTEMIC

In other words, all of your props, and the main line of your sales story, should be in tune with the mood that you've chosen to establish.

To the extent that you can control your sales environment, you will want to ensure that the setting is

appropriate to your strategy. A Plexiglas desk with molded chairs sets one type of mood; leather chairs around a coffee table set another. If you're working in a clothing store, say, do you want the distancing effect that comes from staying behind the counter, or do you want to make every effort to come out into the middle of the room and walk the customer from item to item? When you're visiting someone someone in their office or home, the clothes you wear and the paraphernalia you carry establish a mood. A heavy briefcase suggests a complicated or extremely serious business discussion, perhaps, as might a dark suit with a conservative rep tie.

You have often considered your appearance or the appearance of your environment from other points of view; now look at these factors in terms of the specific mood that you think encourages a customer to buy your product or sign up for your service.

INFECTION WILL REACH A CRISIS

And that's your job. **When you know what you're going for, it's time to go for it.** As quickly as possible, using the influence of your own tempered mood and whatever props are useful, you want to get the customer into the proper mood for a sale.

Don't dawdle, hoping that their mood will run itself down and then you can take over. You don't have time for that. You must take charge, bring their mood in tune, and then strike, before the infecion cools.

Emotions are fragile things; they don't wait around

for you to make plaster casts of them.

Emotions are imprecise: When you're fortunate enough, and skillful enough, to bring out the one that will benefit your sale, strike!

Emotions can be deceptive: A person may look serious or amused, and be feeling something quite different—so you have to get your customer as close as possible to the appropriate mood and tell him that they're feeling it.

Emotions are contagious: To transmit an emotion, you have to feel it yourself. In the sales situation, this should be easy for you, because you have experience with the product and with the feeling it should arouse.

In sum:

> *Rationality is a grand thing, and*
> *most of us think we live by it, when*
> *it comes to decisions like buying.*
> **But emotion is often the most**
> **powerful force.**

When you isolate the emotion that works most effectively with your product—love of speed, appreciation of beauty, increased self-confidence and self-respect, or even plain greed—you can bring extra power to the dynamics of the sales situation by infecting your customer with that emotion. It's the right feeling for the act you mean to instigate!

But your control is not entirely manipulation, as we see next.

CHAPTER FOUR
Letting the Client Tell You
What They Want

Letting the Client Tell You

That's a tricky word, "letting."

Sometimes, in sales, you seem to be "letting" the customer go one way or another, but you are really in control. At other times, you really do want to "let" the customer take lead, because you can learn from it.

To find out what the client wants is, of course, essential to your Power Sales strategy. You may think that you can convince them to *want* something else. Not true. You will be wasting your strengths as a salesperson. The concept is slightly different, but critically so:

> *You will not be aiming to convince the customer to want something he doesn't want; you will be showing him how what you have to sell answers the real desires expressed in what he thinks he wants.*

Try that again.

The customer will think that he wants A. You have B, or, at best, A_2. But what is so attractive about A? Does he want A, or does he want what A represents, or what A is thought to deliver? In other words, can his desire for A, which he thinks is definite, really be answered by what is offered by B or A_2?

- You have to discover the desire behind the want.
- You have to find out what motivates his ideal.
- You have to analyse what his desired product means

to him.
* **You have to let him tell you what he wants—so he will let you tell him what he wants!**

JUST ASK

The most direct way is often the most effective way, in many aspects of the sales process. Ask the man what he's looking for, and if he can't tell you very precisely, then you've learned a lot. It's easier to fill in the blanks than to take a fully formed thought and change it to suit your purposes.

Get all the details you can. The feature he neglects to mention might be the one that becomes a stumbling block somewhere down the road, because you're not prepared to deal with it. It might also be so important to his image of what they want that they take it for granted, as in, "Why, I thought *all* mini-buses came with a built-in bar in the back seat." You don't want them to trip you up with some unexpected demand.

Also, when you get the customer to set out the details, you are getting them to participate in the sales conversation. They are committed to finding, *with you*, the object that is pleasing. The customer is committed to the image that is constructed from a list of details, making another one step closer to making a commitment to buying the product.

And you know where you and your product stand. You have the material to map out your counter-strategy, if your product differs in important essentials from the product that the customer has in mind.

THEN GET HIM TO WEIGH IT

Broken down to its essentials, the product is also broken down conceptually. Each factor might add to the price, or to the lack of mobility, or to inefficiency.

You want to know which are the most important criteria, for two reasons:

- You'll know what kind of thinking is motivating the customer (for example, durability), and
- You'll know which items will give you the most challenge or opportunity.

Don't start eliminating! Go for the positive! Find out what things mean most to him, and then investigate *together* the relative value of each.

For example, suppose you decide that your product will not be able to offer Feature C, or anything like Feature C. You decide that your plan of attack against the item is the cost factor; it's a pretty little thing, but it adds 10% to the cost of the whole product.

Your customer has his heart set on Feature C, and there is no reasonable way to convince him that it is inessential, or unattractive. He knows better. You have to come in from the side, then, agreeing that the feature is a marvel, but suggesting that perhaps the cost makes it impractical. *Gradually, by showing various items from another light, you can change the customer's mind without changing their taste.*

Concurrently, you are emphasizing those factors that your product does offer. Maybe the customer isn't all that hot for Feature K. But it was on his list, and it's a feature that is quite attractive, as presented by your product. Again, you don't want to approach the item from his point of view, which has already ranked it fairly low. *But you shore up his commitment to it by showing how it is a good thing from another point of view.* Perhaps it adds to the life of the product, or prevents children from hurting themselves. **The second quality you bring up will enhance the feature and move it higher on the customer's list of priorities.**

> *By working with the customer, detail by detail, you can change his picture of your product and change the image of the product that he ideally wants—until they overlap each other in most of the critical places*

But you can't work that transformation—which affects his perception of your product and his perception of his desires—until you draw out what he thinks he wants.

SHUFFLE PRIORITIES

When you know what the customer wants, what the hidden desires really are, you may often be able to change his perspective radically. He wants a sports car, but you have a compact van; he wants a fox-fur coat, but you have a good deal on Chesterfields. How can you use your selling power to propel him from one choice to the other?

Find the first priority. Of all the reasons for choosing the sports car, what's the most important? Or, what is the theme running through his list of reasons? Perhaps he likes the flashy image. Let's make it that simple. How, then, do you get a compact van to look attractive to someone who sees himself speeding down an oceanside highway with his hair blowing in the wind.

Well, maybe you can't. If someone really wants a sports car, and you don't have one and won't be getting one soon, then it's good sense for this sales conversation to end.

You don't want to waste your time or their's, when there it little or no chance of being able to satisfy the customer's needs.

But let's say he just *thinks* he wants a sports car, because of all the associations of the good life and trendy style. In short order, you can show how a compact van, in a very different way, has come to be a part of fashionable living. You can mention the people, or the types of people, who now buy such vehicles, and give reasons that resemble your customer's reasons for being attracted to the van.

Moreover, you can give him some of the glamour, too. Perhaps the van can be easily equipped with stereo, or it makes a good camper, or it has a highly regarded German engine. The point is, if your customer thinks he wants a sports car, but you recognize that what he really wants is a vehicle that will bring some snap into his life, maybe you can show the compact van as an example of trendy living which, though obviously not so sexy as the sports car, has *some* flair—and, in addition, has practical advantages as well.

Sound like the treacherous depths of psychology? **Well, the sales professional has to be as perceptive about human nature as anyone else whose job it is to understand motivation and benefit from the knowledge.** You *don't* have to delve into the wellsprings of your customer's desires. You *do* have to recognize them, though, and determine whether or not they can be satisfied by your product or service.

In sum:

You can't sell a product to a zero.

The customer comes to you with expectations, with dreams, with needs, and you are the one who must take that package of desire and direct it toward your product. Finding out what the customer wants will save time, but it will also help you focus your sales strategy. You will have to do some prodding to get all the information you want. You'll be bringing new perspectives to the customer's preconceived notions. **In other words, your** sales conversation will really be a working, thinking relationship, and it may become a little too intense. That's why we should probably talk about the possibility of unintentional conflict...

CHAPTER FIVE
Personality Clashes: How to Handle the Inevitable Occasional Conflict

Personality Clashes

You rub someone the wrong way. . . . How do you smooth things back in the right direction? And where did you go wrong? Or *did* you? Do you call it quits, before your temper gets the better of you?

Maybe he was the one who rubbed you the wrong way. . .and he kept on doing so. **First principles are the best principles: The customer is always right (even when he isn't).**

If you truly are a power salesman, you don't react with anger when a customer gets snappy or begins to contradict everything you say. *You are in control*—and that means you can't be deflected from your sales story. You may back off for a while, and let the customer ride his hobbyhorse, and then, in time, you will bring the conversation back on course.

But some situations threaten to get out of control, and at times you'll have to make decisions about a customer who comes close to being personally abusive. What you do, how you react, will depend upon the situation.

HE KNOWS IT ALL

This is usually a case of your goat getting got, because this type of customer does not *intend* to offend and is not consciously angry with you. He's simply convinced that you can't possibly know as much as he does.

He's read the mags, watched TV reports, talked to experts, and had a bad experience: **Why, then, has he bothered to condescend to talk with you at all?**

That's the key, of course. You let the know-it-all tell it all, because he needs an audience. You may be seething, because of his attitude and because he's got most things wrong or only half-right, but the payoff is in your hands: He's unsure of himself. When he stops, you'll be dealing with a very insecure individual. You'll have to act as if you're talking to someone who is really knowledgeable; you do not contradict him.

Where he is accurate, you can build your sales story. He'll be so relieved that you bought his act that he'll be all the more likely to buy your product.

HE HATES BEING SOLD TO

You may make your first move toward a close, and the customer becomes enraged. He acts as if you've sullied a good relationship. Here the two of you were just having a nice chat, *and you have the bad taste to raise the question of purchase!* Now he knows you for what you really are: a salesperson disguised as a human being! He's not going to let any of your tricks work on *him!*

Well, there's a time and place in everyone's life for "outraged innocence," and this is it—when you're dealing with someone who is hypersensitive to the sales process.

You don't pretend that you're not aiming to make a sale, but you *can* take the position that you were just aiming to please, because he seemed to want the information. **You're in control, but you're not pushing, and you can say so.** You're only there to answer questions and to follow his lead. After all, a really pushy salesperson would have tried to sell him on Product B, which is inexpensive but not really his type of thing. He's more the type for Product C. . . .

HE DOESN'T LIKE YOUR LOOKS

Probably nothing too wrong with your looks. This customer has just had it "up to here," and you're the first available target. He got punched in the eye by someone's umbrella, and someone dented the fender on his car while it was parked, and so on—it's been that kind of day. And *you* are in the way.

Oh, you can get angry. You have every right. *But you are stronger than that.* You are on top of the situation, and you are able to distance yourself from the turmoil this person brings with him. You don't "take it," but you turn it around. His vision is blurred—blurred by real experience.

Your pride is not involved in a situation like this.

> *Where your pride should lie, as a power salesperson, is in the ability to change this customer's whole outlook.*

The day has been bad for him, and he is not acting rationally. You can sweeten the day and bring him back to rationality.

You don't grovel. You don't apologize for what you most assuredly did not do. But you *can* apologize for what *seemed* to be the case. And when you say, "I'm sorry that I didn't seem to be listening to you; I really thought I was." He will be brought gently back to himself and his natural feelings.

It's still true that a soft answer turns away wrath. He's likely to say, if there's no sarcasm in your response, "No, it's my fault. I've had a bad day."

YOU LIED

Just as you're coming to the close, this customer suddenly backs off and says, "Hey, wait a minute. You were talking $450 a month, and now it's $500. Do you take me for a fool?"

Unless you've made such a mistake **(in which case, you admit it *at once*),** this is either an honest misunderstanding on the customer's part or evidence of an overactive distrust of sales personnel. If there's anger in his voice, more than seems to suit the situation, it's probably a case of the latter.

You can anticipate this type of problem by making sure that everything you've said has been backed up on paper, from price to delivery date.

If the customer is being unreasonable, that may be the clue that he's trying to find a way out. He feels trapped, and he's overreacting, because he doesn't have the self-control to admit that, after all, he just isn't ready to buy.

You could choose to become annoyed with this tactic, even when it's not entirely conscious—but that won't get you anywhere. **He's looking for *any* excuse to get out from under the pressure of having to make a decision about buying.** Without realizing it, you have pushed him to the limit (for the moment).

Personality Clashes

You can take him at his word, try to explain that you certainly didn't intend to set down such a disparity—all the while backing off gently from the closing process. You should probably save this person for another day. Just like the one who came in off the street looking for a fight, he, too, will unconsciously recognize that you acted like a reasonable adult in response to his childish fit. If you don't press your luck, he may be grateful enough to return.

In any event, you do not defend your integrity. You have it, and you know you have it. When you're clear about that aspect of your business life, the message gets across. If you got angry, that might be an indication that the customer had hit a sore spot. Honest people don't have to defend their honesty.

The customer is always right.

It's been said before, and it's never been said better. **If a customer leaves in a huff, you haven't done your job.** You do not put him in the wrong, but you keep yourself in the right. You stand on your record, which does not have to be defended. You can take an attack, because you are not wounded by it. Calm and self-confidence—the sense of who you are and what you can do—are your best marshals of defence. They're unbeatable.

Of course, the customer is less likely to lash out at you if he has been well prepared, every step of the way. That's our next subject.

CHAPTER SIX
Client Contact Begins at the Front Desk

Client Contact

Or half a block down the street. . .or with an ad in the morning paper. . .or with the first telephone call made to a prospect. **In other words, the power that triggers a sale must begin to scorch the customer from the very first contact, no matter what form that contact actually takes.** You cannot control all of your "contacts," of course, when we include company advertising on broadcast media or in print, or the appearance of company reps in other situations—but you must take control of every contact with a prospect that is within your power.

How does one get to see you? What are the lures that bring people in or encourage them to dial your number? How do the doormen, receptionists, secretaries, assistants respond to the stranger who approaches you? Does your place of business look forbidding, or is it suggestive of a fly-by-night operation? What does someone first see when they first see you?

Elsewhere in this book, we've talked about the importance of a knockout first impression. You know the psychology by now:

Those first few seconds are several times more important than the next several minutes of an encounter.

Something you do or say may never be erased from the customer's mind.

That holds true for all of the steps that come between the customer's first awareness of you and his actual encounter with you face-to-face.

Remember, by now you've decided what image you have empowered yourself to project in the sales conversation. You've also decided what your convictions are in regard to the product and what it has to offer the people you sell to. And you know what mood you want to establish to nurture the sale, to bring the customer to the climax of your sales story with a white-hot desire to buy. You don't want that mood soured by wrong notes along the way.

STREAMLINE THE TEAM

Whether it's a receptionist, or other salespeople, or an elevator operator—whether it's one person or several that stand between you and your first meeting with the customer—you've got to make sure you're all singing the same tune.

Don't dictate behaviour. But *do* discuss with everyone who greets a customer, or answers a telephone, what you feel should be the unified approach.

Always, you want to emphasize the basic tenets of courtesy and fair play. You want customers, from their first contact with your company, to know that you are not going to waste their time or make them feel uncomfortable. **Everyone on your staff must co-operate in the effort to assure customers that they are not going to be subjected to high-pressure tactics.**

Also, you want to assure customers that they will be seen as individuals. They should be asked for their name, and the name should be passed along. If they have to wait for you, other people in your operation should make certain to keep them occupied. In a well-run business, a junior salesperson can take a customer and begin the groundwork, finding out who the prospect is, what he wants, how he decided to come to your place, and so forth. If this groundwork information is subtly passed along to you, two things have occurred:

- Your job has been advanced, and
- The customer has made good use of his time.

Both of you will be in place.

DON'T LURK

It's a scene right out of *Hamlet:* Too many salespersons working on a floor behave like Polonius—behind the arras, poised in hiding behind the curtain, waiting for the opportune moment to sink the dagger.

In a large retail operation, you may have little control over the look of the store, the layout of your department or the behaviour of the sales personnel. **But you do have control over the most important person in your career: yourself.**

When someone wanders into your department, "just looking," you must interact *immediately* and decide how the relationship should be characterized. Approach and offer to help. If the customer wants to be left alone, leave him alone—*after* ensuring that he knows the layout and knows that you will be available, but not lurking, when he's ready to consider buying.

If he wants your help, get right to the point. If he asks

to look at ties, take him to the tie counter and work your will with him. Don't be distracted, or try to distract him, with the sweater sales along the way. He's explained his needs; you are there to satisfy them. **He won't trust you to help him with other decisions until you are successful with this one.** Once you bring him to the right tie, he can relax. Then, and only then, you can try to direct his attention toward other items of merchandise.

In this situation, you are indicating that you respect the customer's wishes and want to honour them; then, as *quid pro quo*, he might respect your advice and agree to look at some other merchandise.

ENTRANCES BECOME EXITS
The going-away is as important as the coming-in.

Don't just turn away when your business with the customer is completed. Take him to the door, if that's appropriate. He is leaving the place where you are the host. *You* are responsible for his mood, for his well-being, until he is back on the street.

Is there something you should do to make the transition more pleasant, like call a cab, or have someone direct him to his next destination, or have his purchases carried to his car? It's *your* job to see that pain does not enter his life until he is well out of your control.

Obviously, you don't brush him off as soon as he signs, just because another prospect is coming in the door. More to the point, you open up the likelihood of a return visit in the near future.

Client Contact

*You have begun a relationship, not
just made a one-shot sale.*

If he's bought a big-ticket item, all the more reason to
let him know that you will be eager to serve him the
next time around—even if that is five years hence.
Meanwhile, he has family and friends; you want them
to hear that the personal treatment you give a customer
is not only self-confident but suffused with sincerity
and warmth.

In sum:

*Your sales image is not just you the
person. It is affected, for bad or
good, by the entire environment of
the sale.*

What the customer experiences from his first thought
of you or of your product, what he experiences as he
walks through your company toward your office (or as
you walk through *his* company toward *his* office), what
he experiences as these sales encounters come to a
close are all part of his image of you.

*You can't be on top of every little detail, of course, but
that is your goal.* You want to be in control of the customer's entire experience, because you are judged on
the basis of that experience. In that way, and in other
ways, you will be double-checking your performance,
if you want to invest full personal power in your career.
And a checklist can be helpful, as we see next . . . .

CHAPTER SEVEN
Checklist for Client Notes

Checklist for Client Notes

Just some ideas...(Hint: The answer should always be "yes.")

1) Did I stick to my sales story, even when the customer was determined to cover all the details of last night's basketball final?

You can't be rude, but you have to be firm. If the customer really wants to tell sports stories (or whatever), it's not your day to make a sale with him. If you can't get him to focus on your sales story, you have nothing to say.

Don't confuse work in sales with friendship. You're friendly, but only in the service of making a sale. You are at work, and the customer should be at work, too, trying to make a good deal for himself. If not, your story isn't working.

2) Did I make good use of the sales aids available?

Say what you will, a picture is still worth a thousand words (if not more), and something that the customer can hold in his hand gives a sense of the reality of the product. Words and figures in print back up your conversation with unusual strength; books and manuals suggest the power behind your entire operation.

They are not *crutches*; they are *tools*. If they're any good, you're not too good to use them.

3) Did I stress the bad points, or weak aspects, of the product before the customer thought of them?

This always gives you the advantage, this technique of defusing an objection by meeting it before it is actually voiced aloud. You can't make the weaknesses go away, but by bringing them up first, you score two points:

- You present yourself as forthright (always a plus in the sales situation), and
- You control the customer's perception of the alleged weakness, showing how it can be seen more advantageously from a different perspective.

4) Did I try for a close when the iron was hot, or did I wait too long? Did I keep trying, up to the very end of the conversation?

From the very beginning of a sales encounter, you are looking for the opening that begins a closing. Timing is all, but if you mistime, you try again. The desire for a close is like a drumbeat beneath the conversation: try it, try it, try it. You keep circling back to this goal. If the customer is not ready when you first strike . . . .and not ready when you strike again. . .and still not ready when you strike for the third time. . . .you keep striking. This is not baseball. There's no limit to the number of strikes allowed. They stop only when you hit.

5) Did I stick to the positive, even when a negative offered a cheap shot at the competition?

Even politicians are beginning to understand that negative campaigning can backfire on them. **Nobody likes a badmouth!** They may believe the bad news you have about a competitor, but that won't make them feel good about dealing with *you*. You know how that works: the kind of guy who has a wicked mouth about someone else might stab you in the back, too. You don't want to foul the air. Talk about the good things, the wonderful things your product offers. As they say: look at the stars, not at the mire.

6) Did I *help* rather than *push*?

The power selling we talk about is *controlled* power, the kind of power that doesn't have to show itself. **Your strength comes in guiding a customer, in leading him to a decision that he will be glad to make.** Yes, you are in control of the situation, but it is not a matter of whipping a horse into the stretch; it's more like herding sheep, encouraging the desires and needs of the customer to funnel into the decision that is your sales goal.

7) Did I key my presentation to the unique individual in front of me, continually tuning into his unique personality and trying to listen to his distinctive needs and wishes?

You always want to stick to your basic sales story, but it must always be told in the language that is most accessible to the customer in front of you at the moment. You have to listen at several levels, as we said earlier, and you have to build a picture of the life that projects behind the person. You don't change the pitch, but you might change the orchestration.

8) Did I behave with exemplary courtesy, even when I had good reason to be annoyed?

The abrupt salesperson is never right. There is the ripple effect, for one thing: when the customer tells his friends and neighbours about your testiness, he won't neglect to tell them about how he drove you up the wall. And you won't be there to defend yourself. Worse, you will have lost the challenge presented by a "difficult" customer, who may have very good reasons for being difficult.

You can develop the kind of sales power that will transform the testy customer into the reasonable one. This is worth your while. Do it once, and you'll see. You'll never feel as powerful, as "in control" of your own resources, as when you make this miracle happen —and you'll want to repeat the trick again and again.

9) Have I kept the entire sales encounter totally under my control, from facts to mood, shape to conclusion?

If you made a sale, that's fine. *But if you didn't make a sale at the conclusion of a controlled performance, you really haven't established a track record for the future.*

You have to have the method down pat, the method that works for you on good days and bad. That method, as this book means to show, has to be based on a combination of factors:

- Your appreciation of your own talents
- Your precise definition of your own sales goals
- Your ability to read and understand the customers you deal with
- Your ability to devise a sales story with a clear outline
- Your commitment to guide the customer to a sale that will benefit both of you.

In sum:

> *There's a lot to remember, and you will have to keep coming back to checklists like this one.*

Better still, start jotting down your own. You'll know what you need to work on.

And don't, as we see next, forget how it all ends...

CHAPTER EIGHT
The Follow-Up

The Follow-Up

When the customer leaves your territory,the relationship is just beginning: If he bought, he will buy again. If he likes the product, his whole circle of friends and relatives will become potential customers. If he didn't buy, he is still a prospect—and prospects are put on this earth for one reason, as far as you are concerned: to become customers.

If he didn't buy, he's a reminder to you that you have a challenge to tackle; from finding out how you can get to him at last, you will learn a new wrinkle about this unpredictable business called selling.

NET HIM

Be sure you've taken notes about the encounter and can summon up your impressions of the customer with a quick glance.

Don't take passive notes, take notes that lead to *action*. For example, it's not helpful to recall that he doesn't like a particular sport, when you're selling electronic organs; but it might be very helpful to write that he wasn't too pleased with the reedy sound of a certain model. When a new brand hits the floor, advertised as producing a strong full bass, it may be time to call the customer back. **In other words, take notes that will be specifically useful, in a product sense.**

Note down his mood. . .what you thought his price range might be. . .what you really think he's after. These are the things we forget, in a busy life. A stupid call is worse than no call at all; if you call a customer back because you have the vague idea that he might be interested in gold-plated fish knives, but the memory is a corruption of his having mentioned that he keeps prize goldfish, you may have done yourself in.

REEL HIM

As we've discussed in different contexts, **you have a multitude of possible lines of communication that can be opened to any prospect or customer.**
The choice will depend upon your personal style, upon the nature of your business, and upon the relationships that you develop with your customers.
Christmas cards are appropriate, when you are dealing with clients in the trade; if tastefully chosen and sincerely written, they may be correct in certain kinds of retail work.

The rule is: Be the person you are.

The customer knows that you are jogging his memory with seasonal greetings, but he may also be pleased that you see him and his family as worth paying attention to in this way. As long as you remain a professional, those who receive your cards will see you as a professional. You don't go to the extreme of pretending eternal friendship, and you don't veer to the other extreme of mentioning a good deal by name and number. **Propriety is everything.** It is a measure of the respect that people have for you as a sales professional that they expect you to behave with propriety.

There are other kinds of mail contacts, such as notifications of special showings or notices that a product is due for a servicing or checkup. **Want to make a customer for life?** Send a postcard about two weeks before a warranty on an appliance is due to run out. Obviously, if the product is on the blink, he has probably taken advantage of the warranty. If not, he'll never forget this favour. Most of the time, of course, the product will still be working fine. For very little money (and no cost to your company), you've reminded your customer that you care, and that you exist. You also remind him that the product has given good service. Those are three basic reasons for him to come back to you the next time.

ZAP HIM

The telephone is such an important tool of sales follow-up that there is a separate section in this book devoted entirely to Power Phoning.

The telephone is instant intimacy—and that brings both disadvantages and advantages. A phone call puts you immediately and directly in the middle of someone's personal life. When a customer meets you in the sales situation, he is unencumbered; he can concentrate. Most importantly, he's there because he's decided to devote some time and thought to the business of buying your product.

But when you telephone, you can interrupt emotional

scenes, or yard work. You can catch him in almost any mood, with many things to think about. He may be hoping for a quiet evening at home, and there you are...

> *In short, the phone call is, almost by definition, an intrusion.*

If you can prepare him for it, you're better off. You might make a date to telephone him when he leaves your office. Or you might telephone his house during the day, "just happen" to reach his spouse and ask when would be a good time to call. Or you might send a postcard beforehand, saying that you'll call on a certain evening and giving him the option of dialling your phone or answering service (any method that will take him only one try to get through) to beg off.

On the other hand, the intimacy of the phone is often an advantage, if there are no other obstacles. You can concentrate on what the customer is saying, and on what he is not saying. You can get down to specifics, since each of you can focus on words and on how the product looks in words. You can be relaxed with each other, since each of you is secure on his own turf. *Even more important, you can play off the customer's sense of place, because you can suggest how the product will fit into his life, even as he looks around his own home environment.*

The Follow-Up

In sum:

> *There are many different methods of*
> *follow-up. You will know which is*
> *most effective for your situation.*

What you need to remember is to **do it.** A customer is
a comet, trailing a long cloud of possibilities after the
bright star has passed. He can return, and he can bring
others with him—but you have to keep track of him.
You have to ensure that you remain the centre of his
orbit.

All of this advice, of course, goes nowhere, unless
you remember that the power to sell effectively comes
from you, and that the growth of a successful salesperson is a continual, continuing process.

> *Personal contact falls flat, unless*
> *you bring to the encounter the*
> *person that is you, at top strength.*

AFTERWORD

Afterword

Personal Power Sell works on many levels:

- **You go into yourself** and find your strengths, and you determine how they will coalesce to bring customers to the buying point . . .
- **You go to the customer,** using the skills of creative listening and intuition, to find out what makes him tick, where he's aimed, how he can be brought to the place where you want him to be . . .
- **You go into the product,** finding out how it works for you, and for the people you sell to—which aspects make it possible for you to feel conviction that it is a good thing, and which aspects need to be viewed from a different perspective . . .
- **You go into the sales process,** determining for yourself where the lines of force should flow in the sales story—how to build to a climax, when to start closing, how to continue the process into the follow-up period . . .

> *The difference, for you, is that you will concentrate on the motivation behind the rules—the sustained, focused liberation of your powers as a sales professional.*

You want to have personal power, and so you will have it. You want to use it to make sales, and this book will help. *Get that personal power revved up, and you will blaze straight to your most cherished goals in sales.*

PART SIX: POWER SELLING TO GROUPS

INTRODUCTION TO PART SIX
The Many-Headed . . . Friend

A lot of acting is embarrassment; people are embarrassed to do things. Once you get over that, and you can make an ass out of yourself in rehearsal or anywhere, then you have the ability . . .
— Sandy Dennis, actress

Introduction to Part Six

Strong men quail before audiences. You've heard of great heroes who say they would rather face a firing squad than make a brief public address. The pressure of stepping before the public is daunting, even to people who have to do it for a living. You know that many actors or politicians have taken to drink or worse because of the wear and tear of tackling that great monster, the audience.

How can you do any better? How can you turn the tremendous energies fired up by nervousness into maximized power that gets your point across—and turns the audience into a sales-hungry organism, panting for product?

How do you take the sales skills you use every day and convert them into the skills necessary to work a crowd?

That's what this book is all about. In Chapter One, we talk about how one becomes, as the old phrase has it, "accustomed to public speaking." You'll learn how to convince others that what you know about yourself is true: *You have something to say, you know your business, you have something that will bring them pleasure and benefit, and you are eager to make the sale now.*

In Chapter Two, you'll see the group sales encounter from the other side. *What motivates the audience?* What turns them on, and what turns them off? Why should they sit still for you, when there's more action available with a flick of the wrist on the spare TV set? How can you offer—and deliver—more than Joan Collins in living colour?

Chapter Three is a kind of translation exercise. You'll see how your personal tricks of the trade can be used before groups. If you're a "physical" salesperson, practiced in using body language and physical contact with individual customers, can you use similar methods on the platform? *How do you establish the group sales relationship that you typically do when you are selling on the floor and visiting clients in their offices?* How, in short, do you put yourself—rather than a pale imitation—in front of a group?

In Chapter Four, we'll talk about the follow-ups that work with groups. *You have to shift your focus from the group performance to the individual members,* and you have to take your platform personality down a few watts for personal contact. When the curtain goes down, and they're asking for more, you're the one who has to take advantage of the enthusiasm you generate. You're the star, but you're also the order taker.

Basically, Power Selling to groups is just another aspect of what makes Power Selling work for you: the concentration of your unique abilities and aims into one intense effort, coupled with the skills required to draw upon the power generated by the desires and hopes of ten people, or scores, or hundreds gathered together in the expectation that you can bring change to their lives.

All the rules of Power Selling apply, as you will see in the following chapters.

You will be building upon what we've discussed in other books in the Power Sell series—and that means you'll be building upon the self-confidence and *real* selling skills that you have been developing.

Remember: The key to your career in
sales is a better you.

You may be just fine right now, but you can be better; we all can. When selling before groups, as in any sales situation, you are selling what you know. Just as *your product* is improved from year to year—the result of market testing, experimentation, reevaluation—*you* should be improved as you advance toward your career goals.

Introduction to Part Six

What you learn, whether from the power sales concept, or from other sales experts, is only as useful as your commitment to remember it, use it, and review it.

When something works for you, make a note of it; for you should be writing your own book to yourself over the years, jotting down your successes for future reference. *If something doesn't seem to work just yet, circle it in red*....and come back to it months from now, or even years from now.

You're going to be surprised at how much sense our suggestions make. After you've begun the process of Power Selling, assess your own experiences in action, and then come back for a review. Keep reading until the pages are falling out, and you'll be glad you did.

Now, let's walk right out in front of that crowd—**and bring the house down!**

CHAPTER ONE
The Star Power Within

The only person who cares is yourself. So you have to be damned good to get noticed or appreciated! And no excuses!

—Katharine Hepburn, actress

You don't believe us. You know that you will *never* feel comfortable making sales presentations in front of groups. Your knees actually start to knock, and your palms sweat, and your voice goes up an octave and becomes a pinched, dry, unpleasant little sound....

Believe us: Almost everyone feels that way, to some degree, before taking a deep breath, plastering on a grin, and striding out confidently to centre stage.

The difference? They've learned to fool you. They've learned to control the outside appearance, even when the inside is rumbling like a volcano. They've learned to activate the mental power necessary to dominate the physical weakness that comes from nervousness.

But they *are* still nervous. And why not? Nervousness just has to be turned around. **Turn the nerves into verve:** All that jangling energy just has to be properly focused. That hyperventilation is getting your capacities up to top power. Stage fright has you working on all burners—now all you have to do is take that combination of forces, which is shooting off out of control in all directions, and bring it dead centre.

FIND THE EYE OF YOUR STORM

Somewhere there's the foundation from which you can work, the place where you can get your footing and then get the rest in control. It's different for each of us. Some people take control by concentrating on their breathing. Forget the butterflies down below, or the dry lips—these people just cool out on breath control, perhaps aiming for a deep breath every two seconds. Other people find the calm they need by memorizing the first paragraph or so of their prepared speech, concentrating on the pauses after each sentence. If they can just see that opening clearly, they know the rest will follow.

Some people come into focus when they concentrate on their appearance, checking the back of the hair, the amount of cuff showing, and so forth. The point is:

Concentrate on one aspect, and the rest
will take care of itself.

Disaster comes when you flip from worrying about your voice to worrying about the jokes you've planned, from worrying about whether your suit is appropriate...and so forth. **This kind of scattering of your brainpower just contributes to nervousness and emphasizes the chief danger of that nervousness: lack of dead-calm focus.**

GET A RABBIT'S FOOT

A real one is great, if that works—but **many sales professionals, taking their cue from the theatre, have a kind of secret talisman, a good-luck charm, that sets them into high gear.** Usually it's a phrase to whisper to themselves, just before making an entrance. It's a personal starting-whistle. (An actress known for her gentility always whispers, "To hell with them!" before making her entrance. She doesn't hate the audience; what she's saying to herself is, "Be yourself; that's what they came for.") You might want to give yourself a football cheer, or say "Geronimo!" or pray for Mother. Whatever—it's that energy-peaking cry that hits the air before you leap out the plane *with* a parachute. It puts you back in the same place each time: *ready to go, eager to come off strong, determined to succeed.*

KNOW THE DANCE

Remember those little dance instructions showing footprints

taking the proper steps? Well, **you need to know the steps in any public presentation** if (pardon the pun) you want to get off on the right foot.

Do you have stairs to negotiate, or risers? Will you be having to turn to someone to shake hands, before rising, or will you have to make personal contact with audience members as you walk down an aisle?

Chances are you won't just be levered up out of a hole in the floor, so your walk, your ability to interact with the person who introduces you or with others on the platform, even your ability to rise gracefully from a sofa in someone's living room—these simple, ordinary day-to-day actions are magnified, in your own mind and in the sight of others, when you have to perform them in front of people.

The answer? Well, there are two.

First, practice. Even if it's a matter of three steps across the front of a club's basement meeting room, you want to stride, not shuffle. You want to hit the goal, be it podium or just the centre of a room, without having to scuffle around for it. You want your eyes to be doing other things (as we'll discuss in a moment) than peering down to make sure you aren't stepping in something. We mean it: *If you don't have to worry about the movements, you can give attention to the important things.*

Second, stay in character. Yes, you have to decide what kind of walk you want, what kind of stance you mean to take, just as you choose your image in terms of clothes. The cool approach? It begins with the first step, as does the vigorous approach, the combative come-on or any other style of performance.

You are "on" when you're visible.

If you've been slouching in a chair onstage, that's the first impression—the lasting one. Your hip, forceful sales talk will be diminished by this first image. You make your image before a group from the beginning: the way you sit, the way you interact with other people before you speak and afterwards, and the way you walk or exchange handshakes or open your folder of speaking notes. **Sit, stand and speak in character. You are "on" whenever anyone in the room has the opportunity to watch you.**

The performance should be seamless.

YOUR MOST IMPORTANT CUSTOMER?

It's the deaf little old lady in the back row. As you may know, theatrical tradition aims every performance to that mythical playgoer, "the deaf little old lady in the back row."

Make Her Hear

That doesn't mean that you bellow and shriek (unless that's your tried-and-true personal method of choice). It does mean that you have to speak clearly. It means you remember that there's a pause at the end of certain sentences, that you emphasize the important words in your presentation, not *every* word.

Remember: People in a crowded room will turn around to listen when you try to whisper a secret to someone else; if you shout along with everyone else in the room, no one will pay any attention. What keeps the audience awake is not a sustained roar but variety of tone, of rhythm, of mood. *Keep the deaf little old lady diverted, but don't drown her in noise.*

Make Her See

Everything you do, every move you make, should be directed toward her gaze. Your body should be turned in her direction, even if you've moved to the side of the platform to use a pointer with an audio-visual aid. You should always "cheat" towards her, as the stage expression has it, even when you've turned to talk to someone on the platform with you.

When you enter a room or cross a stage, your first step should be with the "upstage" foot, the one farther from the audience, so that your body is aimed toward the audience, even as you cross. When you gesture in profile, you should use the "upstage" hand. *In other words, you are maintaining physical connection with the centre of the back row.*

Give Her Time

When you enter, let your face be seen and studied, and take time with your introduction. Don't present any important facts up front, unless you mean to repeat them again and again. **Remember:** Politicians and other public speakers don't spend a few moments in idle pleasantries because they have time to waste...*they're giving the audience a chance to look them over*, check out the clothes and the hairstyle, get a sense of the personality. A good rule:

> *No one will remember anything you say
> in the first three minutes.*

Fine. That's when you're introducing your image. You're presenting yourself, and your style. You have to enforce these impressions upon the audience, before you can take them to the substance of your talk.

NOW YOU CAN BEGIN

We've just talked you through the beginning because that's probably what you need. The big hump, for most salespeople, is those first few minutes of nervousness. You have to give yourself a routine that will take you through the thick of it—**you have to develop an entrance and an opening that will become so ingrained that they seem to come out by themselves,** and then you kick yourself in the pants and go on.

If you're like most people, the nervousness will pass, after the first few minutes, because you will be doing something that you already do very well: powering your message to people who want to hear it.

No one came to hear you because they hate you and despise what you're selling.... There have been no reports of salespeople being driven from a room with rotten eggs and tomatoes, just because they described a product... Your first-grade teacher is probably not in the audience... CBS has not assigned Dan Rather and his camera crew to cover your sales debut...

So—there's nothing to worry about. *You can do it!*

Correction: **You can do it** *if* **you have prepared yourself properly.**

We want you to be calm in the face of fire, but we don't recommend a foolish arrogance. Those speakers you've seen who make it look easy have worked hard. There's rarely such a creature as a "born speaker." In fact, this creature is about as rare as the so-called "born salesperson."

> *Sales before groups requires special*
> *approaches to preparation.*

Before you begin that talk, you should have certain matters well under control.

Power Has a Well-Defined Shape

Whether it's a 5-minute presentation or a 45-minute demonstration of your product or service, you have to map out the shape—the highs and lows, the climaxes and the anti-climaxes.

Perhaps your product is easily explained, and the purpose of a talk is to build up consumer confidence.

Perhaps there are many features to be discussed, or many possible applications, and your talk will be designed on a point-by-point basis. Still, **there must be a sense of movement, from least important point to most important,** or from the simplest to the most complicated. You are aiming for a climax, even if you have to fake it.

Perhaps your discussion of the product is brief, and you want to spend most of your time working the audience. Even with the question-and-answer format, you must have a shape in mind. You have to take advantage of chance remarks and work them into your design, or you may have to come back to the questioner whose concerns will fit in with your planned climax.

However you do it, there has to be a beginning, middle and end to your presentation.

Power Is Variety

You should plan humour, because it relaxes people (including you). *Shared laughter is a way of acknowledging that we like and trust each other.*

But the humour has to be in the right key. In a three-piece suit before an academic audience, you use wit, not one-liners.

A crowd of retirees is not *likely* to dig pot humour, and so forth.

Think before you quip. Humour reveals a lot. You don't want to play with politics or religious issues, even when you're "sure" of your audience. There are republicans who don't like anti-Democratic jokes, simply because they don't like jokes that take a swat at another group. Get too near the bone with your humour, and you're asking someone to admit to himself, and to you, that he's got a streak of intolerance, or worse.

> *Mild, dull jokes are better than sharp,*
> *clever jokes that can backfire.*

And people don't really mind jokes that have more paunch than punch. *Jokes are a form of greeting, a way of announcing that you all speak the same language.* You're a salesman, not a comedian; you aim for what's pleasant, not necessarily for what makes a "laugh riot."

The same with anecdotes. They should be short, and they should make a clear point. They should have a pleasant tone and never be derisive about another company or another product.

Personal stories? They're fine—*if* you've got someone to help you edit out the fill and the boasting. The personal touch is a way of identifying with your audience, but if your story comes across as condescending, or bragging, drop it. You're selling yourself, yes, but selling yourself as *competent and confident, not self-centred and self-loving.*

Topical remarks, based on the day's news? **Quotations** from well-known writers? **References to films?** Each of these can add variety to your talk, but each has dangers. Remember to consider the tastes and experience of your audience, and the self-image its members have. Remember that you are to share, not teach. *And you don't want to raise controversy where none existed.*

Power Is Eye Contact

Good posture and personal presence are both helped by your ability to establish eye contact. And, as in the one-on-one sales situation, **you develop intimacy by making eye contact,** which can be the door to a customer's innermost feelings.

But be careful. Look, don't stare. *Make contact, don't send out rays!*

If you sense that someone is uncomfortable when you look at him, *slowly* shift your look to another member of the audience. Don't dart around wildly, hoping to settle upon someone who can bear your gaze. In the beginning, as the audience becomes used to you, you might try the old trick of making eye contact with some of the empty chairs in the room or with a point in space, mid-audience. As you talk, you will see who will let you establish eye contact, person-to-person. Above all, don't seize desperately on one poor person who politely returned your glance and address half your talk to him. This will embarrass both of you. If no one will look at you, **don't panic.** Talk persuasively to a cheekbone, or a brow, or a nose.

> *The point is to establish an image of someone talking naturally with everyone at once; you take different objects, light upon them for a while, and then move on to another.*

Power Is Paper

It's said that the legal profession loves paper, and so should you. Even if you like to talk extemporaneously, you can use notes, handouts, forms and other paper props to support your presentation.

Paper shows that you have something in reserve, some more information that you have not yet shared. It shows that you're legitimate, and that you're organized: Everything you're saying must be true, because it's written down. And paper shows that most important thing: that you are prepared to take orders. Paper suggests a history and hints of a future. You may not need it for delivering your sales story, but it can be used as a confidence builder with your audience.

Power Is Solving the Hand Problem

Perhaps the most unsettling aspect of selling before groups is that **our hands, which are essential to so many human activities, are usually worse than useless here,** dangling in an unsightly manner, getting in the way.

The hand problem is important, and you have to solve it in a natural way. President John Kennedy always kept his hands in the side pockets of his sports jacket; the "royals" of Great Britain have learned through the centuries to stand with their hands clasped behind the back; diplomats from the Soviet bloc adopt the military stance of hands stiffly aligned with the trouser seams.

These are recognitions of the problem, if not the most elegant solutions possible. Hands can gesture expressively, *but less is more*, when it comes to having impact. Wild gesturing or repetitive gestures can distract the audience or even become unintentionally humourous. **Worst is when the hands,**

left to themselves, take on a life of their own, undercutting what you are saying. If they start to fidget with pencils or a water glass, insist on straightening your tie several times a minute, leap into your belt loops or seek out loose dandruff in your hair, something must be done. Find your own way of restraining your hands. If clutching a podium seems stiff or unnatural, remember that it's preferable to being *too* permissive with those hands. They have to be suppressed, when not being used to make a point.

One last thing: Let technology be your friend. Today, most people have easy access to video equipment. Steel yourself and make a tape of yourself speaking—preferably in an actual sales presentation. The sound may not be entirely accurate, and your fine figure may be blurred by amateurish lighting, but you don't need a broadcast-quality tape to learn how you come across in a public situation.

- **Is there variety in your performance,** or do you look and sound the same from beginning to end?
- **Do you wave your arms like a windmill?** Do your arms hang rigidly like a dummy's in a store window?
- **Do you look at the people you're addressing,** or do you talk to the floor, to your notes, to the ceiling and to the potted plants in the wings?
- **Do you (be brave, now) have annoying tics,** like hitching up your shoulder or ending every important point with the same kind of smile?

Find your tics before they become bloodsuckers. If you are afflicted with such common verbal diseases as uh-itis, or you-know-itis, or okay-itis, get yourself cured. These verbal habits are not only annoying; they make you look unsure of yourself. You want the audience to be impressed with your information, not to be counting up the number of times per minute you say "you know."

- **Do you have the guts to pause?** Silence is terrifying, when you're the one who is supposed to be filling the vacuum. But the skilful use of the pause can keep your audience's attention where you want it to be, or stress the importance of a specific point, or just give them a moment to think constructively.
- **Do you look like a sales professional in control of himself, of his audience and of his sales talk?**

Now, *that's* the question that sums up all the others!

To help you come to a positive answer, let's go, in the next chapter, to what the audience experiences and sees in a group sales presentation.

CHAPTER TWO
What's in an Audience? Customers!

I really believe that to be a balanced person you can't overdose on your profession.

—John Travolta, actor

What's in an Audience? Customers!

Right on, John. People don't come to a sales presentation to see the salesperson as a caricature, someone leaping up and down as if taking an ego trip on a pogo stick.

What does a group expect? What do they want out of you—and, more importantly, out of your product? Do they want salesperson *qua* salesperson, or do they want a fellow human being who can bring them some good news?

You know what we think, by now. And you know where we think your source of power lies when you sell to a group: You have to know yourself, as in all sales efforts, and **you have to know the group.**

WHO ARE THEY?

There will be thousands of possible situations, and we can't cover all of them, but here are some fairly common examples.

There will be social groups, where you're part of the free entertainment. These people will know each other very well. Familiarity, as you know, sometimes breeds a certain kind of skittishness. In front of his best friends an individual might be less likely to show interest in buying.

You'll have to turn this situation to your advantage: The energy that exists because of the friendships in the room is well-nigh combustible, if you take control.

> *Get a leader to buy, and others will*
> *follow.*

Politely and impressively answer the objections of the club's resident wiseacre, and you've made a sale to the quieter members. *Remember: The social club has a long-standing dynamic that existed before you came and will thrive long after you've made this brief appearance.* Psych out that dynamic—hail-fellow-well-met or socially concerned or whatever—with as much care and focused perception as you psych out the individual customer who walks into your office.

There will be interest groups, where the audience has been brought together by a shared need or concern, perhaps only for a one-time meeting. The focus here will be the product, the idea behind it, rather than the social setting.

You should find out what beliefs or desires have caused the group to be formed, of course. Usually, such a forum requires that you appeal to the head before the heart, if the membership is well informed. *You will want to show how the product or service fits into the overall theme of the group's efforts.* You certainly want to know how the group has reacted to other sales personnel and their product presentations.

And there will be groups formed for a certain age, a hobby interest, a religious connection—in other words, the reason for the formation of the group will not be directly related to your service. *You should never go overboard in trying to suggest that you're an adherent of the group.* No reason why you should know anything about the knight's gambit because you're speaking before the chess club. You're the sales professional; they're the chess players.

There will be trade groups where the emphasis is on *your* product and *your* company's track record.

> *The most difficult of all audiences is a*
> *group of peers, in one way, because*
> *they know the ropes.*

But take the most positive point of view. They understand

what you're facing...and even the most competitive of them will acknowledge a good performance. They're your toughest judges, if you're not prepared, and your most knowledgeable admirers, when you pull off the presentation in your own way.

WHAT DO THEY WANT?

That depends, in part, on who they are, but there are other considerations. What is the stated purpose of the occasion—to give you the opportunity to sell, or to present you as a representative of salesmanship? Are you to explain a product, or a concept? Are you going to make prospects, or actually power the meeting down to the wire of taking sales orders? Are you entertainment, or are you part of a continuing educational effort, or are you there to pay the mortgage—and the group agrees with that aim?

Remember, however: What they want is *not necessarily* what they get!

You take charge of the situation, after analysing it, and turn their script into *your* script.

First, you come to grips with their expectations, and **then** you have to decide how to move them from Point A, where they're sitting, to Point B, where you are determined they *should be*. (And you're going to have to make that move work, even if the audience is already primed to buy—or so you've been told. They may *think* they're where you want them to be, but they probably aren't. You're the only one who knows the target you've set.)

If they are there just for information, you've got to give the information in such a way that they want to act upon it. They thought they just wanted to hear about fire-prevention techniques, but you show them that they need one of your portable extinguishers now, because a fire can break out that very night.

If they are there because they have nothing better to do, then you charge them up with the desire to take your product or service, because it's better than anything else in its class. **People with nothing to do are waiting for action.** You're the action for that half-hour- or hour-long meeting. If you give them zest, they will want to take some of it away. That's why you have a product in your hand.

If they are there because they want to buy something, your work may look as if it's half-done. But the second half, the road to the close, may be even harder. Someone going to a meeting to buy a washer is thinking seriously about buying a washer. They're ready, but they've also been shopping around. They will respond to your most professional approach. They need to know that you respect their intelligence and the work they are devoting to making the best buy. They want you to talk specifics, and they want a certain intelligence in your approach—they didn't just walk off the streets; **they are making decisions and want to be respected as decision makers.**

WHAT CAN YOU GIVE THEM?

No, you don't know the answer to this. You don't know because, like all of us, you have not yet tapped into all the skills and talents that are within you. Oh, at a certain stage of your career, you can say, "Hey, I can give them all the numbers," or "I can tell them which product makes the most sense for their style of living." You probably know when you give people pleasure, make them feel good about themselves, and when you save them money or help them get what they think lies beyond their capacities, make them get more than they expect out of life.

But, *you don't know yet how good you are*—because you haven't tried all the angles yet!

You know what you can bring to an encounter with a blue-collar worker who walks into your showroom and would like one of the new, lighter pickup trucks, or to a vice-president at a nuclear-power plant who needs cooling towers that are more efficient. That's the one-to-one you work with every day.

But groups demand a different kind of skill, as we've seen. You have to be more *concentrated* upon your image, because it is being scrutinized by many pairs of eyes—and what one misses, another will catch. Yet, you have to *disperse* your attention, because the whole, or the group, is made of many parts, each an individual.

You have only the barest clue, when someone sits there silently and laps up your every word. Will she, or won't she?

What do you do? You become every person you are. . . . you run up flags, and see who salutes.

Let's say you mention the economical features of your product—take note of who's listening and play to her and her friends. Or when you talk about the fresh style or the top speeds, see who takes a bite. Or when you talk seriously about the possible disadvantages of your service, who is listening intently?

You won't be able to play the audience like Toscanini the first time out, or even the first few times. The tough truth is:

> *Things worth doing well, things worth doing better than your competitors can do them, take hard work and practice.*

But you'll discover that sales power before groups comes

from the desires of the group. *You can give people what they want, as soon as you learn to recognize who wants what!* You can help the person who is afraid to make a sizeable investment, because you are prepared to explain how the investment will make sense in his life. . . .or you can help the person who is afraid of taking a step that will change his personal style—the smaller car, or the wider tie—because you have already learned how to ease these changes.

Think about these important points:

- An audience is composed of individuals.
- Each individual is someone very much like someone you have dealt with before.
- There are no surprises, if you get close enough.
- You speak to the audience, but you listen to the individuals.
- You project a powerful personality on the platform, a focus of attention for the group—but you simultaneously *give* in another way, by picking up on the reactions of individuals.

It may actually be easier than it sounds. While you're speaking, each member of the group thinks of himself as anonymous, a person in the crowd. *You're* in the enviable position. *You're* in the spotlight; you have the personality that is pulling together the combined energies of the room. The individual member of the crowd doesn't think you are paying any attention to *him*. . . .

In fact, you are delivering your speech or presentation with such expertise—*you are so solidly on top of your material*—that you are constantly watching the house.

It works. If you've never addressed a group before, you'll be surprised at how much you see. You learn who is attached to whom, and who is really interested, and who laughs at which type of joke, and who looks worried when you mention the price. . . . and on and on. Once you have your presentation under control, you never want to put yourself "on automatic" and lose spontaneity; nonetheless, you will be able to watch as you perform—your audience none the wiser.

It is by means of that watching that you decide what to give your audience—how to play them, how to bring them to the point of sale.

You will give them your best, we know. But better than that, by watching them, you will be able to give them *what they need, what they want, and what gets you closer to your goal.*

WHO ARE YOU?

As John Travolta warned us, you can't become nothing but a selling machine before a group. *You must be a human being. You must be a sales professional*, proud of what you do for a living and proud of your progress in your field, but *you must also be the person you are*, just as you are yourself—at highest pitch—in one-to-one sales encounters.

This is today (in case you forgot), and whatever your political point of view, you have to agree that the people who succeed here are the people *who are people*. Presidents become the most powerful leaders in the world because they seem like regular guys. . .and movie stars make millions because they seem to be not *too* different from the girls and boys next door to all of us. . .the culture heroes of this democratic society are those with talent who don't act as if they've dropped from a gilded cage.

You're playing to the same audience. In order to give confidence you must demonstrate expertise, but you can't come across as a know-it-all, or sales will be few and grudging. Customers want to *like* the people who sell to them. They want the sales relationship to be a friendly encounter. Life has stress enough without an additional dollop from you.

Yes, you want to project the power and self-confidence that we think are essential to Power Selling. **But you also want to project the you that people will like and trust.**

You want people to understand that you can tell them the truth about the product, because you live a life that is characterized by the same concerns and problems that bedevil theirs. You want to allow yourself to reveal vulnerability, when that's appropriate, because you are not a machine, but a human being taking on a challenging job.

You want to consider any question raised by a member of the group, as if you've never heard it before: Ponder it, look at it from more than one side, and then give an answer that calls upon your personal and professional knowledge. (**Warning**: Within reason, it's good to develop some answer tricks, to give you time to think. "I'm glad you asked that," is an old favourite of politicians who would like to disembowel the questioner for raising the issue; you can come up with even better ones. But don't let such devices become your undoing! If you rely upon them, they begin to sound false.)

And you want to show yourself to be the kind of person who is not going to cut and run. Your anecdotes should suggest that you keep in contact with former customers, or that customers become your friends. What could be more persuasive than a story about how a product or service has changed the life of a customer—obviously (and you don't have to say it), you have kept in touch.

This chapter has reviewed four major expectations that any group or audience is likely to have:

What's in an Audience? Customers!

- They want you to know who they are—and to respond.
- They want you to figure out what they want—and respond.
- They want you to make clear what you can give them, and suggest that you're willing.
- They want you to be yourself—in bright lights and big letters—so they can see you and decide for themselves what you're made of, and how far they can go with you.

Those are tremendous expectations, of course. *How will you meet them?*

- *By drawing power from the expectations projected upon you* and turning that force of curiosity and desire into the wish to buy
- *By drawing power from the unexpressed hopes of the people sitting so attentively in front of you*—even when they do not really believe that this meeting would bring anything important to their lives
- *By drawing power from the resources you've developed* for selling, for giving, and, finally
- *By drawing power from the bright lights of your own true personality.*

> *Selling to groups is a matter of meeting their expectations, and going beyond them. It's a matter of pulling together a cumulative force from the aspirations of individuals.*

And it's something you've done before. . .as you learn in the next chapter.

CHAPTER THREE
Been There Before (Sort Of)

Luck to me is . . . hard work—and realizing what is opportunity and what isn't. I think knowing what you can not *do is more important than knowing what you* can *do.*

—Lucille Ball, actress

Been There Before (Sort Of)

Yes, there are limitations when you sell before a group.

You won't be able to press the flesh, if that's your style, or ask the customer about his favourite football team, if *that's* your style. **You have to translate.**

It's like the actor making love to an actress on the stage. If his experience is in the movies, with the miking in close and the close-up lens, he is used to imitating a real-life experience. Put him on the stage, and he has to project, because 3,000 people have paid to hear each murmured word, and he has to exaggerate his facial expressions, because they have paid to see emotion at work on his famous features.

You're in the same boat, when you speak to groups.

*You have to translate your sales
techniques from the one-to-one
encounter to the demands of the group.*

First, as Miss Ball suggests, you have to clear the air by deciding what you can*not* do in the group sales situation.

You don't play to one individual, at the expense of the group impact. You don't limit your appeal; you have to broaden it. You can't depend upon feedback, so you have to wing it. You can't walk offstage to look up prices, or make a better deal with the boss; you're stuck with your game plan.

You can't bring the customer into immediate contact with the product. You can't suggest that the customer call a spouse for a consultation.

You're on your own!

But, there are ways of translating your best sales assets from showroom or client's office to platform.

You begin by noting down what you do best, what gives you the feeling of being in control of a sales encounter.

- **Are you most solidly in control** when you can take the customer to the product and give him the hands-on experience of its features?
- **Do you do your best work** when you can discuss the technical aspects of your product, or do you prefer to talk about how it will be useful to the customer's style of living?
- **Do you employ body language** in your sales work, or do you depend more strongly upon the use of verbal language?

*See yourself before showing yourself to
a group!*

It's your responsibility to plan a sales strategy for group presentations that accurately reflects your own achievements as a salesperson. There are some rules, however, that will work for everyone:

THE MAN'S BUSY

And so is the audience.

You've learned in one-to-one sales to gauge the customer's time. You know how to keep him long enough to inform him, to heat him up, to persuade him and to get him to the point of signing the sales slip, but you also know that you can't keep him too long.

Don't try to fight the clock when you've got a captive audience. Say your piece, and end it. **A crucial aspect of getting on the stage is knowing when to get off.** Leave, while they're asking for more.

If you're to speak for five minutes, so be it. If you're to speak for forty-five minutes, and the coughing level rises, or chairs begin to scrape musically against the floor, or audience members begin to show signs of incipient narcolepsy ...then *stop!* No matter how much time you've been allowed.

It's a strange thing, but true. *The very people who are terrified of appearing before groups are often the ones who, once started, can't bring themselves to stop.* Maybe they just can't believe how much fun it is, and they become exhilarated.

Don't make that mistake. An audience is not as passive as it looks, just because people are still sitting down. They can be seething inside.

GIVE 'EM CANDY

So they won't have to stare at your face the whole time.

Films, slides, charts—anything that will add visual appeal will be appreciated.

You may be a Michelangelo of words, able to paint in unforgettable detail the portrait of your product, but make it easy on the audience! **When you are selling on the floor, you have the product right there.** You can pull it apart and show the interior; the customer can stroke it, or kick the tyres.

For group sales, you have to come up with an equivalent. If you are lucky enough to work for a company that has produced sales films or slide presentations, don't be too proud to use these aids. If the photography isn't glamorous, you can build your talk upon that defect. If the voice-over sounds like some underpaid announcer who doesn't understand what he's reading, you can build from that.

Even a defective film presents pictures.

And pictures are a tremendous psychological tool. There is

the product, larger than life, and there is the context in which it's being used, so the audience wants to buy the context, too, by buying the product. They want to buy the juicer because the juicer is being used beside the kidney-shaped pool in Trousdale Estates, California. That kind of association, if it's available to you, is invaluable.

No film or video? You can easily make charts that will help you, with photographic blow-ups of your product. *Use your imagination!* Produce charts that reflect the uniqueness of your own sales approach. You might have pictures of yourself at work, with a customer at your elbow. You could show yourself dismantling the product, or repairing it. You could be talking with people in the field who are using your product. *In other words, inexpensive 35-mm prints of you in action—you as salesperson who knows his job and tends to business on several levels—can show the audience what they won't hear if you just tell them.*

Despite what you might think:

Show *is more important than* Tell.

And there's much to be gained from bringing parts of the product, if you can't bring the whole thing—a swatch of leather from the buttery soft seats that distinguish your luxury automobile, say, or an actual handset from the telephone system that could revolutionize the work of an office.

Nor should you miss an opportunity to demonstrate what the product does, if that's appropriate. If it slices fresh oranges, you have fresh orange slices to pass around the audience. The good taste of the fresh fruit will reflect upon the worth of your slicer.

BAD NEWS/GOOD NEWS

*It's even more important before a group
to defuse possible negative feelings by
bringing up possible disadvantages of
your product before anyone else does.*

Think about it: A couple of people, knowing what you represent, have probably already mouthed off about the problems someone claims to have had with your product, or about its relatively high cost or bad maintenance record. They're waiting to get you, and the audience may know that.

You can take that negative power, which is lying in wait, *and transform it in a flash to positive vibes,* by bringing up the objections yourself. The reaction will delight you.

If one customer, given this approach, begins to trust you for being so straight with him, think of the heightened effect when a whole roomful of people can turn to each other and nod their heads in appreciation.

They thought you might be caught off guard, but you walked right in and turned the disadvantage to advantage.

Of course, your prepared script will explain why the disadvantage should be seen from another perspective, or should be balanced against the arguments of the real advantages.

A group is a minefield, if you make the mistake of trying to hide something. There's always someone there who has heard the worst, and is willing to bring it up. Not even Caesar's wife would give a press conference, since no one is above suspicion these days. And with consumerism at its high-water mark, you can be sure that any bad press, or weak product ratings, will be on tap.

Take the challenge, and then you can sail into the good news. Your questioners will still be recovering, as you charge ahead, and your good points will seem all the brighter because of your skill in wiping away the allegedly bad points.

TACK TO THE WIND

Is the economy weak? Then you talk about savings when a customer walks in. Are interest rates about to rise? Then you tell him about the advantages of making a buying decision *fast*.

In these situations and others, you go on the assumption that your customer, an individual who lives in a society that has its economic ups and downs, will be responsive to certain society-wide economic pressures.

So too with a group. In the audience situation, an individual is more likely to admit to himself that economic pressures are affecting his purchase, because everybody else is subject to the same kinds of pressure.

Never forget that people read the newspaper and watch TV news.

Your group may not play the stock market, but they will feel better about their own buying power when the Stock Exchange has been rising and the media have been publicizing this show of investor confidence. Your group may not invest in the dollar market, but they will realize what a strong or weak dollar means to their daily purchasing power.

You have to take the prevailing winds, whatever they are, and turn them to your advantage.

And you have the herd instinct on your side. Everyone in the room will agree that, say, the economy is in a decline, and food prices are too high, and the real estate market looks insecure....okay, then what? If you let the herd stampede, the conclusion might be to put your money in a sock under the bed. But you are the one with the whip hand, and you must be prepared to turn the herd in a more profitable direction.

You take the prevailing views, discuss them briefly, and then you show how the situation suggests that *now* is the time to buy from you.

However you design your argument, you will have a room filled with people who agreed with you about the state of the economy; *the trick is to keep them with you as you move on to further agreement*—the economic advantage of deciding to buy *now.*

KEEP THE CAMPFIRE GLOWING

You are telling a story when you make a presentation. We have already noted that your script should be planned out in detail, if not word-for-word. It is a basic tenet of power selling face-to-face that you **never deviate from that script;** it's dangerous to improvise.

It's 100 times more important to stick to your tried-and-true story when you're facing a group. It's the spine, the structure, the shape.

See if you can put into one sentence the basic storyline of your sales presentation. It could be, "Our new oven will enrich your family life by freeing you from the tedium of cleaning it every week," or, "Our lawnmower, though expensive, will save you money by lasting for a lifetime and save you effort by picking up the grass by itself."

No, Shakespeare has nothing to worry about—but your competitor does, if you can make your story appealing, brief, believable.

The whole talk or presentation is derived from that basic story line.

Of course, you tell this story to a customer; the difference, in front of an audience, is that you tell it once, in a straight line, and dramatically. You can't keep coming back to the points that a customer doesn't get the first time, because you don't have that kind of feedback.

And remember:

> *The good storyteller is the one who has his audience asking, "What happens next?"*

Don't give everything away at once. Build from the beginning to the end. *Save the best for the last.*

BE A SNAPPING TURTLE

Strike when the irons are hot. Come to the point when the audience is ready to hear how they can buy. Be prepared to take orders, and let them know that you can deliver *immediately*—if not sooner.

With some personalities, it's successful to start asking the audience for a show of hands of who's interested in buying. For obvious reasons, that can be a tricky turn. If only a hand or two is raised, some unwanted humour is injected into the occasion.

When you close in the showroom or in a client's office, you can try, and try again, and then make it happen.

Much of the same kind of thinking works with an audience, but few salespeople are comfortable with the revival-meeting approach, coming back again and again to ask for people to raise their hands or step forward.

Been There Before (Sort Of)

You have to sense when the audience, or some of its members, have got the message and can be powered into action. Then you have to decide what method of closing is most effective for you. But, most of all, you have to be prepared to take orders.

Long lines make short tempers . . .
and reduce sales!

Be sure that you have a system set up, in case there is a large audience response to your presentation. It's usually a good idea to take an assistant along. One of you will be writing up orders; the other will be answering questions.

If it's impossible to streamline the process of taking orders, you can soften the experience by bringing along refreshments. Or you can take names and telephone numbers and promise to contact these people as soon as possible.

Obviously, it is ideal—just as it is in the one-to-one sales situation—to get a signature on the dotted line *immediately.* Think of every method to effect that, short of making people waste their time waiting in a long line. Bring along several assistants, or design an abbreviated sales slip just for such occasions—**but aim to get that signature, and get it without inconveniencing the buyer.**

Even if waiting in line isn't the most unpleasant experience in the world, most people do it too often and are immediately turned off by the thought. Besides, you don't want to have the look of the assembly-line salesperson. It won't fit the image of personal warmth and individuality that you've worked so hard to project from the platform.

Make sure that order-taking will be brief, pleasant, and efficient.

Don't spoil the pleasure of your presentation by leaving a

bad taste in the mouths of the very people who've risen to your challenge!

In sum:

> *The sales techniques you use with an*
> *audience are very similar to the skills*
> *you practice every day.*

- Don't forget what you know; just open up the focus.
- Don't fear that you're out of your depth, just relax and paddle.
- Don't become a different person; just expand what you are.
- Don't think an audience is bigger than you; it's made up of people who are depending on you.

And you still know everything that brought you this far.

But is it a one-night stand?

Shouldn't be. In the next chapter, we talk about the follow-up procedures you should use with groups, and couple of other hints about making yourself effective on the platform.

CHAPTER FOUR
When the Show's Over

Nobody has pride in what they're doing; they just want to show a little profit.

—Barry Goldwater, U.S. Senator

When the Show's Over

You don't cut and run, because you have pride in what you do as a salesperson—that's a given.

Cut and run? Well, some inexperienced speakers don't realize how strong a commitment is implied when they address an audience. *You may not have intimate contact with each individual, but each individual has intimate contact with you.*

You were giving a talk, but the members of the group were hearing you talk to them. Each person in the audience has a right to feel that promises made were promises made *to him*. If you said, "Come on down and see me," you'd better mean it—and you'd better be prepared to deliver in person. Your discussion of the product, your answers to certain objections —anything you said was registered by the individuals as individual responses.

You have a responsibility to your audience—and they are a new opportunity for you.

THE RESPONSIBILITY

You can't possibly remember everyone in the group, but you should **take full notes about the event and keep them in your office.** Who introduced you, and was someone given an award, or did someone sing?

Whenever you can, *send thank-you notes to everyone who participated in the meeting.* They may not have done it for your sake, but thank them anyway. They paved the way for you, and you have reason to be grateful.

Later, when someone from the occasion calls or comes by, *you will be able to put him in context.* If you have the chance to check with your notes, you will be able to "recall" some event or some person by name as a conversation-starter. That will put you both back into the glow that was produced by your talk.

It will also help you remember exactly what your sales story was that night. Perhaps prices have changed since the appearance, or a model has been discontinued. It's *very* important for you to know what information the customer is working with, so that you will both understand each other. Otherwise, it may seem that you are changing the story you told earlier.

Did you make some special promise to the group? Whether it was a 10% discount, or a free calendar, you'd better come through, even if the sands of time have run to the bottom.

In short, the individual who comes from the group has already had one sales contact with you. That contact had a certain shape; you gave a certain story; certain opportunities were presented. **This meeting, then, is not your first,** even though the two of you have never chatted face-to-face.

*It is a meeting based upon the promises
and expectations of the first.*

That is the tricky thing to remember about prospects who have heard you talk. *So far as they are concerned, a kind of sales relationship is already established.* If you were good, then you came across as a real human being, and they may almost have the impression that they actually talked *to* you that night.

You have to build from the talk, as if it had been a personal encounter between you and this member of the audience. Otherwise, you are in danger of angering or upsetting the customer and, as you have every reason to recall, *he* *is not one man but part of a group.* You do not want him returning to them with an unpleasant story about salespersons who sound plausible on the platform but turn out to be something else in person.

Turn down the volume—bring in the camera. Perhaps you don't need the warning, because you're secure in being yourself. In any case, don't rev up to the magnified personality you used on the platform when a member of the group happens by. That was for the needs of the occasion, for the demands of public performance. Now, you can be yourself.

THE OPPORTUNITY

What *kind* of opportunity depends upon the group.

The Mailbag

If possible, get a mailing list. If you're speaking to buyers in your industry, this is a given; it may be more difficult if you're talking to a men's club. But ask. Explain that you don't mean to invade anyone's privacy, and that you don't mean to weigh the postman down with useless third-class mail—you are just a salesperson who will send a postcard now and then. **And stick to that promise!**

After a few days, while your talk is still fresh in everyone's mind, send a very brief note to all members of the audience. You want to thank them for their kindness in listening to your story so attentively. You want to repeat your offer to help them. You want to emphasize—in a very few words—why now is the time to buy.

This is an inexpensive method of personalizing your appearance. You show that you care about the audience; you were not just a one-night stand but have opened the possibility of becoming a presence in their lives.

You exist! You are not just a creature on the stage. You were not just a performance (yes, that's the danger in appearing on the platform); you were a working salesperson and, as the note or postcard should prove, you are hard at work right now.

The Telephone

Whole books have been written on the use of the telephone for sales. Remember that there are pitfalls in telephoning:

- You have to have a fine ear for the other person's response.
- You have to be very careful not to call at the wrong time.
- You have to know the rules of etiquette for the region you're telephoning.

All that said, the telephone is an immediate way of contacting someone. It is a powerful instrument for making a sale, or making an appointment that will lead to a sale.

When you telephone after a presentation before a group, you are in a special situation. Certain people, if they've been impressed with your ability to present yourself before an audience, will be nonplussed when you call. You seem larger than life to them, perhaps—not quite a movie star, but still somebody who can do something that seems frightening to them. You will have to allow for this reaction and bring yourself—or your image—back down to normal size before the call will become very productive.

Everyone, however, will know who's calling. That's a tremendous advantage. You've been introduced to scores of prospects without ever speaking to them directly—but they know who you are.

*To mix metaphors, you already have
your foot in the door when you call.*

You have something to talk about (because you saved your notes from the meeting), and you have business already started, because you've already made many of the sales points that would be the substance of the usual prospect call.

Therefore, a telephone call to one of the members of the group is a *closing call,* **by definition.**

They've heard you at your best. They know the story, bad and good.

Now, you just have to get to the problems that may be keeping them from buying. You use all the tricks of professional closing—taking for granted that they want to buy—explaining how you have already prepared a delivery, if they are ready, listening to every answer but "no."

The Flesh

When you can't make a close over the telephone, you get the prospect to agree to come see you, or to invite you to his home. *(This, too, is the aim of the mail approach.)*

You transformed yourself from personal-contact salesperson to performer on the platform; now, you work a similar transformation on the member of the group, from passive audience member to customer actively participating in the sale. **You want him primed to become your co-conspirator in perpetrating a purchase.**

When he comes face-to-face, you have the opportunity to bring out all the tricks that you could not really use on the stage. You will be showing him a whole new side of your personality:

- **The charm you radiated** for a whole audience can now be beamed directly at him.
- **The expertise you demonstrated** can now be ignored, because he doesn't need it, and you can concentrate on those aspects that piqued his interest in the first place.
- **You can direct your techniques** to his personality.

In all of these ways, you are still drawing from the impression you made before a group. To this individual, you are still a little larger than life. **You are in the power position,** because you took the risks that so many people are afraid to take. You exposed yourself on the public platform (even if it was just in a corner of someone's living room while a few people had coffee), and the individual from that audience is still impressed.

Take advantage and run with it.

ONCE A STAR

Going public with your sales techniques is going to change your life in some unexpected ways.

The Boys in the Locker Room

When you speak before your peers and competitors, or before a group of buyers in your industry, you're going to learn a tremendous amount—if you can take it.

> *No matter how good you are, you can be better, and the best friends you have are the ones who will tell you where you were strong and where you seemed weak.*

Listen. That's all. Don't take offense. Don't get your defenses up, even if you know that a criticism *isn't* offered in the finest spirit of comradeship. *You don't care about the spirit of the criticism; your job is to fire up the spirit which will take you past the weakness.*

If it takes an "enemy" to tell you that you muffed a close, or you didn't make a sales point clear, that's a good enemy to have. Cherish him.

You don't want to trade good feelings in the short term for diminished success in the long term. Take the hurt now so that, in the future, what you get are praise and sales orders.

Take a tip from professional actors, who say:

> *The good reviews don't help, because they don't give anything to work on; the bad reviews, if they're specific, can make possible some significant improvements.*

The same is true for you. Be grateful that people tell you you're a living wonder in front of an audience. That's kind of them. But be on the lookout for the person who will admit that maybe—just maybe—you should think twice about some of the jokes you use, or should number your points, so they're more easily understood and remembered—or whatever advice will help you sharpen your presentation.

In short, speaking in public is going to change the nature of your relationships with fellow professionals.

The Streets and Byways

Once you start speaking before groups, you give up a

large degree of privacy.

Before, you may not have been noticed if you snapped at a rude bank clerk. Now, someone may see you. Oh, sure, you may have dealt with hundreds or thousands of customers in your store, but things change after you've been on a platform. It's part of the phenomenon.

Think about it. Customers rarely recognize most salespersons on the streets, because they're out of context; they're not standing in front of a rack of video cassettes, and so they look vaguely familiar, but that's all.

When you speak, though, you're the focus of attention on a bare platform for a concentrated period of time. For several minutes or much longer, the members of the audience see nothing but you and perhaps a sales aid or two. **After that, you will be recognized,** and the recognition can be positive or negative.

After you begin making public presentations, you should **remember that your public image is in your power.** If you were dynamic and neatly dressed on the platform, but show up at the supermarket, hungover and wearing your bedroom slippers, someone will notice. So what? So the 10, or 50, or 100 people who remember your stunning performance are likely to hear about your appearance at the supermarket. Why? Because you now have *news value* to them.

That's right. You were an event, and that brought you contacts and sales. It also set up a network of people, many of whom you wouldn't instantly recognize on the street, but who instantly recognize *you.* You are part of their social history. **You are going to have to keep yourself clean.**

Well, that's no problem. You *want* to keep your act clean. You want to project in your daily life the same kind of confidence and command that you were able to project before a group of your fellow human beings.

When the Show's Over

That's what you want, and the fact that you are more visible will help you remember that that is what you want.

You brought yourself to the sales presentation before a group, **and now that experience will reverberate in your life,** strengthening your resolve to be the person you are, **every minute of the day.**

The Career Curve

Taking the plunge into group selling may cause you to reconsider your career plans:

- Is this avenue more successful for you?
- Would this approach be more useful if you handled a different kind of product?
- Does it open up new possibilities for your work within the company?
- Does it whet your desire to expand your operations?

Moving out into the community is bound to put you into contact with new people and new ideas. You are out there to sell, to make your presentation in your own way—but you should be listening, as well. From groups you may be able to get the lay of the land more clearly than from a series of conversations with individual customers.

The challenges of selling before groups will put you to the test, in many ways, but they will also give you opportunities to broaden your own horizons. Be open to them.

In sum:

> *You're going to love the experience of selling before groups. It is a great boost to the ego, and we all love that.*

It is a fascinating opportunity to meet many different types of people, and we never met a successful salesperson who wasn't interested in people. And the pressure will really give you a good overhaul, tightening your weak points and polishing up your most dependable skills.

Trust us, because people who get past the first five minutes of selling before a group really *kick into high gear and thrive on the challenge.*

Trust us, because the skills you develop in selling before groups will *make you a more powerful and controlled salesperson* in every other sales situation.

Trust us, because you will never realize the depths of your own personal power as a sales professional until you *conquer the difficulties of selling to groups and feel the thrill of winning,* before the eyes of others.

AFTERWORD

I take a simple view of living. It is keep your eyes open and get on with it.
—Sir Laurence Olivier, actor

Afterword

There's no more exhilarating power than the sense of bringing whole groups of people around to your point of view.

Power Selling, of course, is just another way of persuading other people that your view is the right one—that they can benefit from your product or service...that they will be happier with their lives if they buy your product...that they need your product.

The power comes from the focused attention of others, in part, *but it also comes from the concentrated need in the room.*

Audiences want to be entertained, and a group sitting down to listen to a sales presentation wants to be sold. If they don't know that about themselves consciously, you know that about their unconscious and you can bring out those desires and satisfy them.

You have no reason to hesitate.

You are not just one person; you are the focus of sales power, the skilled professional who can bring together all the disparate forces in the room and channel them into sales.

They want **you to sell to them, and** *you want* **to sell to them.** If these two things are true, what can possibly prevent sales from taking place?

Only one thing: *a faltering in the stretch.*

You must remember that Power Selling requires follow-through. You have to summon up your energies to make that first important entrance. You have to concentrate your skills upon telling a story that makes your product desirable. You have to stay alert for the cue that indicates it's time to begin your close.

But the power must stay on full strength to the end, and beyond.

You leave the audience wondering how it could all be over

so soon, and how they can have some more—and then you continue the performance in the days afterward, through the mail or telephone or personal contact.

Power Selling before groups, then, does not begin and end with the actual presentation.

It comes in the preparation, which can take a lifetime, and it continues through until the last member of the audience is sold, and sold again. And sold again.

The Power Sell before groups is not just
a 30-minute show; it is a career.

TALK AND GROW RICH
The apprentice millionaire's handbook
Ron Holland

How often have you tried and tried to remember some elusive fact that hovers just out of reach, only to find that when you've given up and stopped trying, the information simply pops into your head? This is Ron Holland's amazing formula: SSS — silence, stillness and solitude at work.

Here he describes how SSS can be used to discover ways and means to acquire anything we desire, simply by talking to people. He demonstrates:

- How to persuade people to do what you want, but have them think that it was all their idea.
- How to sell anything to anybody, including the most hardened and demanding buyer.
- How to generate so many fool proof ideas that you will need to carry a pen and paper around with you to write them all down.

This book truly is the handbook for all Apprentice Millionaires.

Paperback
ISBN 0-7225-1955-9
U.K. £4.99